Meet the
Dancers

Meet the
Dancers

FROM BALLET, BROADWAY, AND BEYOND

Amy Nathan

HENRY HOLT AND COMPANY
NEW YORK

Photo Credits

Childhood photos: All photos of the dancers when they were young appear courtesy of the individual dancers, except the following: p. 2, © Martha Swope; pp. v, 70, © Rosalie O'Connor; and p. 140, © Lance Cheshire.
Other photos: Front cover, pp. ii–iii, 8–9, 11, 13, 140–41, 150, © Marty Sohl; back cover *(top)*, pp. i, vi *(bottom)*, 1, 22–23, 28, 118–19, 121, 125, © Andrew Eccles; back cover *(bottom)*, p. 15, © Rosalie O'Connor; pp. ii *(second from bottom)*, 30, 58–59, 61, 68, 70–71, 77, 79, 145, © Paul Kolnik; pp. ii *(bottom)*, 106–107, 109, © Tom Caravaglia; spine, pp. vi *(top)*, 174–75, 178, 185, Eduardo Patino, courtesy of Co.Dance; front flap, pp. vii *(top)*, 46–47, 55, 137, 188–89, 192, 196, © Joan Marcus; pp. 34–35, 37, 39, Geoff Winningham, courtesy of Houston Ballet; p. 44, Pam Francis, courtesy of Houston Ballet; p. 49, © Nan Melville; pp. 82–83, 85, 90, © Stephanie Berger; pp. 94–95, 103, © Ken Friedman; p. 98, © Peter DaSilva; p. 115, © Lois Greenfield; pp. 152–53, 159, Paul Talley, courtesy of Southern Methodist University; pp. 164–65, 169, © Jared Redick; p. 167, © Jo Cardin; p. 200, © Hidemi Seto.

Henry Holt and Company, LLC
Publishers since 1866
175 Fifth Avenue
New York, New York 10010
www.HenryHoltKids.com

Henry Holt® is a registered trademark of Henry Holt and Company, LLC.
Text copyright © 2008 by Amy Nathan
All rights reserved.

Library of Congress Cataloging-in-Publication Data
Nathan, Amy.
Meet the dancers: from ballet, Broadway, and beyond / Amy Nathan.—1st ed.
p.   cm.
ISBN 978-0-8050-9787-0
1. Dancers—Biography.   2. Dance—History—20th century.   I. Title.
GV1785.A1N37 2008   792.802'80922—dc22   [B]   2007027589

First Edition—2008 / Designed by Meredith Pratt

P1

A portion of the proceeds from this book will go toward promoting dance education.

FOR CARL, ERIC, *and* NOAH

INTRODUCTION
Dance On 3

Gillian Murphy
BALLET DANCER,
AMERICAN BALLET THEATRE 9

Clifton Brown
MODERN DANCER, ALVIN AILEY
AMERICAN DANCE THEATER 23

Lauren Anderson
BALLET DANCER,
HOUSTON BALLET 35

John Selya
FROM BREAKDANCING TO BALLET
TO BROADWAY 47

Teresa Reichlen
BALLET DANCER,
NEW YORK CITY BALLET 59

Amar Ramasar
BALLET DANCER,
NEW YORK CITY BALLET 71

Lauren Grant
MODERN DANCER,
MARK MORRIS DANCE GROUP 83

David Leventhal
MODERN DANCER,
MARK MORRIS DANCE GROUP 95

Sarah Wroth
BALLET DANCER,
BOSTON BALLET 165

Nick Florez
L.A. DANCER 175

Nancy Lemenager
BROADWAY DANCER 189

GLOSSARY *201*

RESOURCES *211*

ACKNOWLEDGMENTS 217

INDEX *221*

Julie Tice
MODERN DANCER, PAUL TAYLOR
DANCE COMPANY 107

Glenn Allen Sims
MODERN DANCER, ALVIN AILEY
AMERICAN DANCE THEATER 119

Elizabeth Parkinson
FROM BALLET TO MODERN
TO BROADWAY 129

Aesha Ash
FROM JAZZ TO BALLET
... AND BACK 141

Jamal Story
FROM MODERN TO BROADWAY,
BY WAY OF THE STARS 153

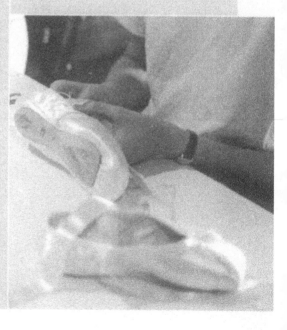

Meet the Dancers

John Selya (front), around age thirteen, with ballet superstar Mikhail Baryshnikov dancing right behind him in an American Ballet Theatre production of La Sylphide.

Dance On

Introduction

I'm always amazed at what kids can accomplish when they throw themselves into something, and there can be no better examples than the sixteen "kids" you'll meet in this book. They're all grown up now and have become successful professional dancers. Some perform in ballet or modern dance companies, while others are kicking up their heels in Broadway musicals or strutting their stuff in music videos. But it all started when they were dance-crazy youngsters, sweating their way through dance class, day in and day out, as they (and their aching muscles and oh-so-sore feet) did what had to be done in order to master the intricate technique, expressive beauty, and exhilarating joy of dance.

In this book, these pros explain how they got hooked on dance. Many fell in love with it at a very young age, but others didn't discover dance until they were teenagers. You'll read about the ups and downs they experienced along the way. For some, those challenges were especially hard to take, as they came to terms with the fact that their bodies didn't fit the stereotype of a classical dancer.

A few even experienced burnout as kids, having started dancing very early and then finding that they needed to pull back and take a break. That happened to John Selya, seen having the chance of a lifetime in the photo on page 2. He was dancing with superstar Mikhail Baryshnikov in an American Ballet Theatre production of the classical ballet *La Sylphide*. Then John decided to quit! Feeling stressed out from too many classes, he did other things for a while. However, before long, he realized he couldn't live without dance and came back, full-steam ahead.

Like John, many dancers in this book had other interests as kids, enjoying such activities as swimming, riding horses, playing soccer, acting in plays, making music, competing in gymnastics, or curling up with a good book. These activities broadened their experiences and helped make them the exciting performers they are today. But for many of these pros, being involved in extra activities slowed down during their early teen years. By then they were

SUGAR PLUM SIGHTINGS

The ballet *The Nutcracker*—with its Mouse King, toy soldiers, Sugar Plum Fairy, and dancing candies—played a big part in the childhoods of the dancers you'll meet in this book. Most performed in this holiday classic as kids, but four didn't. Being turned down for a *Nutcracker* production actually helped one girl find her way in dance. As you read on, be on the lookout for who was or wasn't in this winter wonderland of a ballet.

taking so many dance classes that there wasn't time for much else. "Dance is so time-consuming," notes modern dancer Julie Tice. "I had to give up a lot in high school. I couldn't go out for sports, cheerleading, choir, or anything like that." Every once in a while, that got her down. "But then I realized there was nothing else I wanted to do as much as dance."

Ups and downs continued for some well into their professional careers, as they changed companies or, in some cases, even changed dancing styles. A few are nearing the time now when they may have to start winding things down a bit. A full-time performing career for a dancer doesn't last forever. The wear and tear of dancing can take a toll on the body. Some of these pros are planning ahead for the day when they may have to stop performing regularly.

To choose the dancers featured in this book, I asked for suggestions from major dance companies and also from a prominent dance agent, Victoria Morris. I selected these sixteen dancers because they followed different paths in their training and in their careers. There are, of course, many other possible paths that can lead to a life in dance, but the experiences of these sixteen give an idea of what it takes to excel. Despite the differences in their journeys, however, they have some things in common. As kids, they all had amazingly supportive families, with enthusiastic parents and other relatives who spent countless hours driving or accompanying their talented young dancers to classes, rehearsals, and performances. They also had encouraging teachers to guide them, both at small, local studios where most started out, and also at the more advanced, professional-level schools that many attended later.

Most important, taking all those dance classes—and coping with aches, pains, spills, and sprains—was something these dancers did as kids because they absolutely adored dancing. "I was sort of shy, but when I danced I felt completely free," says Gillian Murphy, now a principal ballerina at American Ballet Theatre.

This love of dance continues to carry them along. "Dancing looks very glamorous onstage, but there's a lot of work you have to put into it," notes New York City Ballet's Tess Reichlen. Professional dancers, like Tess, continue to take class every day, no matter how famous they become. They log in long hours of rehearsing, performing, and exercising, followed by the always-important icing down of sore feet, ankles, and muscles. They also periodically check in with physical therapists to deal with the injuries that are bound to happen. As Tess points out, "If you want to go all the way, you have to really love it."

Tess, Gillian, John, Julie, and the other pros you'll meet in this book really do love it. So do many other dance students who try their hardest but don't manage to make it as professional dancers. It's like basketball: Only a few basketball-loving kids grow up to play in the NBA. This book's dancers lucked out and made it to the top. They learned a lot during their journeys. On the following pages, they share valuable tips that can help smooth the way for kids who are just starting out in the exciting and demanding world of dance.

DANCE TALK   STYLE STORY

Ballet, modern, jazz, hip-hop, tap—these are some of the main styles of dancing studied by the pros you'll meet in these pages. At the start of the glossary (on page 201), you'll find descriptions of these styles, followed by definitions of other terms you'll run across in the book. However, to gain a real understanding of a type of dance, you have to see it. Photos can help. So can watching dance on TV or checking out dance videos, such as the ones listed in the resources section (page 215). Better yet, go see live performances by professional companies or contact local dance studios to find out if you can observe various kinds of dance classes or see an upcoming recital.

Gillian Murphy thinks her fearlessness in ballet may have come from playing soccer as a kid—and also perhaps from the belly flops she loved doing off the diving board.

Gillian Murphy

BALLET DANCER
AMERICAN BALLET THEATRE

Grew up in: Florence, South Carolina (born in Britain)
Age she started dance class: 3
Dance schools: Local studios around Florence; Columbia (South Carolina) Conservatory of Ballet; North Carolina School of the Arts
Studied: Ballet, modern, creative movement
Pets she had as a kid: Dogs named Pepper and Patch; cats named Orange, Calico, and Black
Favorite books as a kid: Books by E. B. White and Roald Dahl; Lord of the Rings series
Other activities as a kid: Soccer, swimming, fishing, running, cello lessons (briefly)
Class she takes now: Ballet
Other activities now: College courses, reading, teaching dance, Gyrotonics exercises, going to concerts and operas
Pet she has now: Cat named Selah
Music she listens to now to relax: Reggae, country, classical, opera
Professional career: American Ballet Theatre

"When I was in kindergarten, I'd wear out my sneakers walking on my toes, pretending they were pointe shoes," remembers Gillian Murphy. She was too young for real pointe shoes, the hard-toed slippers ballerinas wear, but she liked dancing around the house as if she were a ballerina. She had started taking dance at age three with creative movement classes in Belgium, where her family lived for a while. "My mother put me in those classes as a fun activity. We learned basic ballet positions and did things like run around like butterflies. I enjoyed it." So when her family moved back to the U.S. in time for kindergarten, Gillian began taking real ballet classes at a studio in her South Carolina hometown.

"I enjoyed the challenge of ballet, learning something new in every class," she says. But she liked other things, too. She lived near a lake and went fishing a lot. She also loved to swim, especially doing belly flops (ouch!) from the diving board. When she was seven, she started soccer. "At first, I was the only girl on the team. I wasn't that good at it, but I really loved it. I enjoyed all the running around. I also liked playing with my older brothers and their Star Wars figures. I was a big bookworm, too. When I get into a book, it's like I'm lost in a different world."

When people asked what she wanted to be when she grew up, she'd say, "Doctor, marathon runner, and ballerina." But right before her tenth birthday, her plans

Gillian flying high as she dances the role of Cinderella for ABT.

changed. That's when she tied on pink satin pointe shoes for the first time in ballet class and began dancing on her toes for real. "I was a little young to start pointe, but almost instantly I felt comfortable in them. There is an initiation process with pointe shoes, of getting blisters when you first use them. It's painful. But you get used to it. I loved the floating, ethereal feeling of dancing on pointe. That's when I totally fell in love with dance. My dreams of being a doctor or runner died as my dream of being a ballet dancer took over."

"COMPLETELY FREE"

By the time she started on pointe, she had switched to a different studio in her hometown and was taking class about four days a week. Her favorite part of class was doing big jumps and turns, not surprising for a kid who enjoyed belly flops. "I was sort of shy, but when I danced I felt completely free," she says.

As she became more involved in ballet, her soccer career ground to a halt. "My parents were worried that I'd get clobbered because I was small for my age and boys on my team were getting big. I was sad to give it up. I think soccer developed a fearlessness in me." She would need that sense of daring for the challenges of ballet, especially the whopper of a challenge she set for herself when she was eleven. That year, she had to select a dance to do at an arts festival. She picked something nobody expected an eleven-year-old to try: the dance of the black swan Odile from the classical ballet *Swan Lake*.

"I was aware that it was not totally appropriate for me to do that at such a young age, but I took it very seriously," says Gillian. She had videos of *Swan Lake* and loved watching famous ballerinas

---

CLASS-Y TIP

<u>GRIN AND BARRE IT:</u> "When I was little, I got bored with barre work," says Gillian. That's the beginning part of a ballet class when dancers hold on to a wooden bar to do exercises. "I understood it was important, the building blocks for everything else. But I wanted to get into the center to do jumps. Now I treasure barre work as a meditative part of warming up. There are so many things to work on every day at the barre: your hands, your arms, trying to go beyond yourself in every way." Franco De Vita, the principal of ABT's Jacqueline Kennedy Onassis School, adds, "The brain can understand an exercise easily, but body memory is not so fast. We repeat an exercise not to be boring but so your body knows it exactly."

As Odile, Swan Lake's *black swan, Gillian still nails all thirty-two fouettés, but she explains, "At that point in the ballet your legs are totally wiped out, so it's always a challenge. You're tired. It's a matter of perseverance. I know I can do it, and I just keep up with the music."*

do amazing jumps and turns in this ballet. Gillian was determined to master the black swan's tricky moves, including the role's thirty-two rapid-fire, nonstop fouettés (a difficult kind of turn). "My teacher gave me the key to the studio, and I'd go in with my mom or dad and make myself do an extra fouetté each day. My dad suggested that if I pulled my arms in a little, I'd speed up and make it easier to keep going. That helped. I also thought of it as doing four sets of eight, telling myself: 'If you can do eight, you can do eight more.'" At the performance, she nailed all thirty-two fouettés, a big achievement for a youngster from a small-town studio. "This was something I wanted to keep doing."

"THE RIGHT PLACE"

To keep soaring in dance, Gillian needed more demanding training than was available in her town. So she hit the road, as did many dancers you'll meet in this book. They started at small studios near home, but when it was clear how talented they were, their families searched for more advanced training. Switching studios often meant big sacrifices. For

---

INSIDE SCOOP
BEING A PRINCIPAL

GOOD POINTS: "Being a principal dancer in a ballet company is an honor, a dream come true," explains Gillian. "When I was promoted to principal, I didn't think, 'Oh, now I can just coast along.' I saw it as a new beginning, a chance to create something special of my own. I've had incredible roles to challenge and inspire me."

BAD POINTS: "There's a lot of added pressure. As a principal you're expected to carry the evening." At ABT, different principals perform the same role on different nights of the week. Audience members often come to see performances based on which principal is performing, and the company keeps track of which one brings in the biggest crowd. But Gillian explains, "Those pressures invigorate me to push myself further."

Gillian as Odette, the swan who dies of a broken heart, with Ethan Stiefel as Prince Siegfried, in ABT's Swan Lake.

Gillian, age twelve, it meant driving with her mom more than an hour a day after school to take class at the studio of the Columbia City Ballet in Columbia, South Carolina. The next year, she actually moved to Columbia with her mom and little sister. Her brothers were away at college or boarding school. Her dad stayed home with the family's dogs and cats. This arrangement was tough on everyone, but they were willing to pitch in because of Gillian's love of dance.

Soon she was dancing in Columbia City Ballet productions, sometimes performing on weekdays during school. That didn't please teachers at her middle school. "They didn't understand why I'd skip school to perform," Gillian says. "It made sense to find a school where academics and dancing were part of the same schedule." She found it, thanks to her dad, who had just started a new job in North Carolina, which has an excellent arts high school, the North Carolina School of the Arts (NCSA). It's a public boarding school that offers regular academic courses, such as math and science, along with outstanding dance training. She auditioned, was accepted, and planned to start ninth grade there in the fall.

However, she almost changed her mind. That summer, she took ballet classes in New York City at the School of American Ballet (SAB), the dance school of New York City Ballet. She had found out about SAB's summer program from a notice in *Dance* magazine. SAB officials were so impressed with her dancing that they invited her to stay on after the

---

PERFORMANCE POINTER

GETTING IN CHARACTER: "The purely technical part of dance isn't the main point of a performance," says Gillian. "Performing is about sharing the moment with the audience, sharing the emotional development of the character." Of course, she practices a role's steps until she has them down, but she also thinks about "what's going on in the character's mind. In *Swan Lake*, the black swan doesn't think she's being evil. She's just on a mission to deceive Siegfried. Think about what the character wants. That creates a feeling in the performance. I enjoy getting into a character. The limit is your imagination, which should be quite boundless."

summer and spend her high school years there. "It was tempting to stay in New York, but my parents felt that going to school in North Carolina would not only be more practical but also a more nurturing environment. After starting at NCSA, I realized I was in the right place."

"THRILLED"

Her main ballet teacher at NCSA, Melissa Hayden, had been a star dancer with New York City Ballet. "She was incredible, a challenging teacher who stressed having a solid core of pure technique, not too stylized," recalls Gillian. Most days Gillian would take ballet early in the morning, followed by two regular academic courses (such as history or English) before lunch; in the afternoon there would be another ballet class, a few more hours of academics, and then rehearsals. Once a week Gillian took a modern dance class, during which she set aside the straight-back stance she used in ballet in order to master the more flexible movements of the upper body that are called for in modern dancing. She enjoyed the dance classes and regular academic classes, too. "Classes were small. That helped me come out of my shell and talk more."

Gillian performed a lot at NCSA, often doing pieces that had been choreographed for New York City Ballet by one of that company's founders, George Balanchine. She was also the Sugar Plum Fairy in the school's

Nutcracker each year. In addition, she entered competitions; she was a finalist in the Jackson International Competition in Mississippi and a winner at the Prix de Lausanne in Switzerland. "I realized ballet is an art and not a sport to be judged. But performing in a pressure situation at a young age in competitions is a good experience. It definitely helped me. It's also inspiring to see so many talented kids."

As wonderful as NCSA was, "after three years it was time to move on. I took extra courses to graduate a year early and thought I'd go somewhere like the San Fran-

TYPICAL DAY

Here's a typical day for Gillian Murphy during rehearsal period:

10:15 to 11:45 A.M. — Company class at ABT's studio

12:00 to 3:00 P.M. — Rehearsal

3:00 to 4:00 P.M. — Lunch

4:00 to 7:00 P.M. — Rehearsal

Company class is the class that dance companies have for their performers. At ABT, it's a ballet class, and Gillian takes it every morning, both during rehearsal periods and when she's performing. "We rehearse five or six days a week," explains Gillian. On performance days, she may have a few hours of rehearsals but likes to have enough time between rehearsal and performance to take a nap. One night a week she stays on at the ABT studio after rehearsal to take a college course. On days off, she might get a massage or take a Gyrotonics class, an exercise system that helps keep her muscles in shape.

cisco Ballet School for more training." Then someone from American Ballet Theatre (ABT) came to her school and saw Gillian in class. "She pulled me out of class and said I should go to New York and have ABT artistic director Kevin McKenzie see me. I was thrilled!" ABT, based in New York, is one of the world's best ballet companies.

Gillian went to New York City a few weeks later, in early spring, to audition. Her audition consisted of taking a class at ABT while Kevin McKenzie watched. Then he offered her a job in ABT's corps de ballet, the large troupe of dancers who usually perform in a group, as a background for a ballet's soloists.

However, he wanted her to start right away. "I can't join now," Gillian told him. She was really eager to finish her courses and graduate from high school. She asked if she could join a few months later, after graduating, a gutsy request for a seventeen-year-old to make. Luckily, he agreed. She joined ABT that summer.

"BRANCH OUT"

"I had never danced in a corps de ballet before ABT," says Gillian. She had always been a soloist or a principal, dancing alone or with a partner. "As a soloist, you can play with your timing a little. But if you're dancing with twenty-three other people in the corps, you have to be exact.

SUGAR PLUM SIGHTINGS

Gillian Murphy was in her first *Nutcracker* at age six, as an angel in a show in her hometown. At fourteen, she was the Sugar Plum Fairy at NCSA and has performed that role ever since, often as a guest artist with companies around the country.

It's not easy. It took a few months before I felt comfortable with this." While in the corps, she was chosen to do some soloist roles. Before long, she was promoted to full-time soloist. Then, at age twenty-three, she was promoted once again and became one of ABT's principal dancers, the highest level of dancer in many ballet companies. "As a principal, you can really dig into the characters."

One ballet she has dug into with gusto is the one she started learning as a kid, *Swan Lake.* Now she performs both Odette, the good swan, and Odile, the cunning trickster. "They gave me several months to work on *Swan Lake* before performing it. You need to make it look effortless, graceful, and magical." She has done modern dance roles too, both at ABT and as a guest with other groups. "It's so important to be a versatile dancer. It's great to branch out and do modern works."

She is branching out in other ways as well. She teaches in a summer dance program, Stiefel and Stars, organized by her boyfriend, ABT dancer Ethan Stiefel. She also takes college courses in her spare time in such subjects as art history and physics through a special ABT program. Professors from Long Island University come to ABT's studio to teach the dancers after rehearsals are over for the day. Other dance companies also have programs that encourage their performers to take college classes. "I want to earn a college degree," Gillian explains. "I enjoy the courses. It helps my dancing. The more you grow as a person, the better you are as an artist."

DANCE TALK   **STUDIO-SWITCHING**

Many dancers in this book did some studio-switching when they were young, often starting, as Gillian did, at small studios near home. It's important to find a studio with teachers who are good with kids. Clifton Brown (featured in the next chapter) had a teacher at one studio who yelled at kids and made them cry. "I don't feel that was helpful," says Clifton. "We left that studio." His grandmother found a better one by keeping her ears open at competitions, hearing what people said about other studios. Nearby colleges and dance companies can also offer suggestions.

After a few years, Gillian and Clifton moved to studios connected with professional dance companies. Both later attended arts-oriented high schools. These specialized arts high schools aren't only for students who aim to be pros. "We use dance to help you discover who you are and to open yourself up to ways to use the lessons of dance for the rest of your life," notes Doug Long, a counselor at a private arts high school, Interlochen Arts Academy in Michigan.

However, many dancers in this book didn't go to specialized arts high schools. A few were lucky to take dance at their regular schools; others received all their dance training outside of regular school. To find out about dance academies, arts high schools, and studios affiliated with professional companies, check out the listings in dance magazines. (See resources, page 213.)

*Clifton Brown at about six with a medal he won
for dancing to a rollicking ragtime tune, "The
Entertainer," by Scott Joplin.*

Clifton Brown

MODERN DANCER
ALVIN AILEY AMERICAN DANCE THEATER

Grew up in: Goodyear, Arizona
Age he started dance class: 5
Dance schools: Local studios around Goodyear and Phoenix;
School of Ballet Arizona; New School for the Arts;
The Ailey School/Fordham University Bachelor of Fine Arts program
Studied: Acrobatics, tap, jazz, ballet, modern
Pets he had as a kid: Dogs named Pepper and Fifi
Favorite book as a kid: *Where the Red Fern Grows*
Other activities as a kid: Guitar and organ lessons (briefly)
Classes he takes now: Ballet, modern
Other activities now: Sudoku puzzles, working out at a gym,
teaching master classes
Music he listens to now to relax: Jazz singers
Professional career:
Alvin Ailey American Dance Theater

"I was clumsy as a child," says Clifton Brown, who would sometimes trip or bump into things when he was little. "My grandmother wanted me to do some sort of after-school physical activity to help with co-ordination." There were two places in their Arizona hometown where he could do this: a karate academy and a dance studio. His grandmother let five-year-old Clifton watch a class at each and decide which he liked best. "I wasn't so interested in fighting," he says. But he loved the tumbling and flips he saw kids do in an acrobatics class at the dance studio. And so a new dancer was born.

"I took acrobatics at that studio for a few months, and then I got into a combo class of tap and ballet. After a year, I was taking jazz dance, too," he says. "I liked tap best for a while. Then I started liking ballet more." He always loved jazz dancing, with its flashy moves and snappy, strutting steps done to cool pop tunes. He also loved performing in recitals and in dance competitions. He was only six years old when he won a prize at a national competition in Las Vegas. "I did an acrobatic routine to the theme from the movie *Rocky*. My mom made my costume: a flesh-toned leotard and boxing trunks with stars and stripes on the side. It was fun." Clearly he wasn't clumsy on the dance floor!

Besides improving his coordination, dance helped in another way. "I was very shy as a kid. I still am. Dancing was an outlet for self-expression, a way to get your feelings out through dance."

"FLIPS ON THE PLAYGROUND"

Clifton stayed at that local studio a few years, taking class two or three afternoons a week. Then he switched to other studios his grandmother found. She hadn't known much about dance before Clifton started taking class, but she began checking around to find out which were the better local studios. Gradually she came to realize that good ballet training was important for any dancer. The best ballet instruction in their area was at the School of Ballet Arizona in Phoenix, a half-hour drive away. When Clifton was ten, she started driving him there every afternoon. He took ballet class there five days a week through the end of middle school. But he missed the sassy fun of jazz dancing. So while he was in Phoenix, he would also take jazz dance at other studios in the city.

"I did homework in the car on the way to and from Phoenix," he says. "I did pretty well in school, but if my grades dropped, I couldn't go to dance until I brought up my grades. In dance, you're constantly learning choreography and so you figure out how to learn things quickly. That helped with schoolwork." Something else from dance helped in school: "I'd do flips on the playground, and guys were kind of impressed." That might explain why Clifton didn't get teased much for being a dancer.

PERFORMANCE POINTER

PEP TALK: "There's a certain degree of nervousness that happens with any performance," says Clifton. He still feels a little nervous before an Ailey performance. "It helps to be well prepared. When you're prepared, you feel more confident." If he finds he's getting too nervous, he gives himself a pep talk. "I say to myself, 'Okay, I've rehearsed this a lot. I've gone through it in my head. I know what I'm doing.'"

INSIDE SCOOP
BEING IN A MODERN DANCE COMPANY

GOOD POINTS: "At Ailey, we do so many types of dance that you can stretch yourself as a performer," says Clifton. "When we repeat a piece for a while on tour, the more you do it, the more new things you can find in it." Glenn Sims, another Ailey dancer you'll meet in this book, adds, "We travel around the world giving performances. That's something I always wanted to do, see the world."

BAD POINTS: Seeing the world can be exhausting. "We're on tour nine months a year. Living out of your luggage can be hard," says Glenn. Clifton adds that with dances the company does a lot "it's hard sometimes to find ways to give a fresh performance. I tell myself that every night is a new audience and this may be the only time they ever see the company. It may not be new for us, but we have to do our best all the time."

All those dance classes meant there was no time for sports or other activities. He didn't mind. He was having fun dancing and winning prizes at competitions. "I did competitions all through high school. They were good experiences. You win some—you lose some. I saw them as performance opportunities and chances to see other dancers."

"ARMS LIKE MINE"

However, one part of dance class was tough for Clifton: the corrections that teachers gave him about his arms. "When I was twelve, my arms were much too long for my body," he explains. "My arms are still long, but at that age my arms were awkwardly long. I was having a hard time controlling them. I was always getting notes from teachers that my arms were sloppy. I didn't feel there were many dancers with arms like mine."

Then he checked out a video from the library that showed performances by The Alvin Ailey American Dance Theater, one of the top modern dance companies. A dancer in the video—Donna Wood—had very long arms. Clifton was astonished at how she moved them, especially in a piece called *Cry*, in which she danced alone on stage. Her arm movements were graceful and flowing at times, but at other moments they were angular and powerful. With her arms, she expressed a whole range of feelings: anger, pain, heartache, love, pride, dignity, and hope. "Her arms were so extremely long, but it was amazing the way they moved," remembers Clifton. "Her port de bras [arm movement] was so beautiful and so expressive. I thought, 'Oh, so that's how you use your port de bras, how you support it.' That inspired me." From then on, he understood better what to do when teachers said, "Fix your arms."

That video gave Clifton his first look at the Ailey company. In addition to *Cry*, the video showed the company's most famous piece: *Revelations*, which is set to spirituals and depicts both the sorrowful yearning as well as the joyful spirit of the African American experience. All the dances on the video were choreographed by Alvin Ailey, who founded the company in 1958. His pieces use a mix of styles, from sassy jazz and moody modern dance moves to the graceful elegance of ballet. It's soulful dancing that can be both mellow and explosively athletic. "His dances brought together so many of the things I wanted to be able to do," says Clifton. Also, nearly all the company's dancers were African American. That appealed to Clifton, who had always been one of the only black students in his dance

Clifton dancing in the Alvin Ailey American Dance Theater's production of Shining Star, *choreographed by David Parsons.*

classes. After watching that video, this twelve-year-old knew what he wanted to be one day: an Ailey dancer.

"WONDERFUL DANCING"

During high school, Clifton finally had a chance to learn the kind of expressive modern dance that he saw on that Ailey video. He went to arts-oriented public high schools in Phoenix where, along with English and math, he took dance as part of the school day, studying modern dance, jazz, and also ballet. "I liked the freedom of movement in modern dance and jazz. But I kept up with ballet. I wasn't interested in being a classical ballet dancer, but I wanted to be able to do the amazing technical things that ballet dancers can do."

Clifton was still dreaming of being an Ailey dancer, but his grandmother had her heart set on him going to college. Luckily, the Ailey company had a special program with Fordham University; students could study dance at The Ailey School while taking academic classes at Fordham to earn a college degree. In his senior year in high school, Clifton applied to this program, which held auditions around the country. Clifton auditioned in Houston, Texas.

At the audition, students took a dance class while Ailey officials watched. The first part of the class was ballet; the second part was modern. "Then I did a two-minute solo I had worked up,"

SUGAR PLUM SIGHTINGS

At age ten, Clifton was the prince in a production of *The Nutcracker* at Ballet Arizona in Phoenix.

Clifton cradling Dwana Adiaha Smallwood in Acceptance in Surrender. *To the right behind him is Kirven J. Boyd; to the left is Glenn Allen Sims, a dancer you'll meet later in the book. The three men are guardian angels for the woman in this piece, which was choreographed by three other Ailey dancers.*

Clifton recalls. "I got some good feedback right away. The Ailey people said, 'Wonderful dancing. We hope to see you in New York.' I was so excited." He was also accepted into Ailey's summer workshop. Right after his high school graduation, Clifton headed to New York City.

"IN THE MOMENT"

"The first time I saw the Ailey company perform live was during my first year in New York, when I was in the college program. The dancers were amazing. I finished one year of college. Then I quit. I didn't want to just take class. I wanted to perform professionally." So he auditioned for the dance troupe he had dreamed of joining for so long. He was only nineteen, but he was well-trained and ready. He managed to win a spot in

TYPICAL DAY

Clifton's schedule during rehearsal period is similar to Gillian Murphy's: a ninety-minute company ballet class in the morning, followed by six hours of rehearsing, with an hour off mid-afternoon for a late lunch. About three days a week, he goes to a gym before company class to do weight training, which helps with all the lifting he has to do of both male and female dancers. If he injures himself, he checks in with the company's physical therapist. "For anything besides normal muscle soreness and cramping, I go to the physical therapist. There's always one who travels with us when we're on tour. I have an ankle injury that comes and goes. When it's acting up, I'll ice it."

the company, becoming the youngest Ailey dancer that year. What about his grandmother's college dreams? "She wanted me to at least try college and then if I decided I didn't want to do it, that was okay," explains Clifton. "I can always go back later and finish getting the degree."

In his performances with Ailey, Clifton uses a range of styles: ballet, modern, and jazz. "It's good I studied so many kinds of dance as a kid. There's a lot of variety in the dance world now, with more demands placed on dancers." To keep up with those demands, he takes class every day. Usually it's company class, which at Ailey is often a ballet class because it's such a good foundation for the kinds of dancing Ailey performers do. Clifton can also take classes in modern or jazz that are offered at The Ailey School. In addition, he works out at a gym a few days a week.

What he enjoys most about being a dancer is what he loved about it as a kid: having a chance to express his feelings. "When you feel like nothing else exists, when you're very much in the moment, just dancing, it's magical."

AUDITION ADVICE

WATCH, MARK, DO: In auditions and competitions, judges often watch you take class to see how well you learn new combinations of dance steps. "Try to be in the front row so you can see what's going on and so the judges know you're eager to be seen," advises Clifton. "But don't be pushy. If judges see you push in front of someone, that won't make a good impression. Then, the first time they show a combination, *watch*. Don't do it. If you try to do it, you'll miss something because you're not watching. Be still and pick up as many details as you can. The second time they show it, *mark* it. That means not doing it full out. Don't do the legs fully. Do it in your mind and your arms so you start to get it in your body. Then, the third time they show it, go ahead and *do* it."

DANCE TALK   **TAPPING TOES**

Like Clifton, many dancers in this book started with tap, including Tess Reichlen, a ballerina you'll meet later. She says, "I really liked tap. It's fun and helps you learn about rhythm and timing." Franco De Vita, principal of American Ballet Theatre's ballet school, agrees, "Tap is fabulous for musicality and coordination of the feet."

Quite a few of the dancers also started when they were very young by taking creative movement classes, which put an emphasis on having fun with dance rather than learning technique. "I think it's good for young students to take creative movement, to understand early that dance is expressive, rather than getting the message that there's a right or a wrong way to move," notes Martie Barylick, a dance educator at Mamaroneck High School in New York State.

Jazz dance was also a popular way to begin. "We have many students who started out taking jazz and tap before coming to our school," explains Shelly Power, associate director of Houston Ballet's Ben Stevenson Academy. "The repertoire in ballet companies is becoming broader. Ballet dancers need to do jazz and modern so they are more marketable to a wide group of companies. To accomplish this, we teach ballet as our main discipline, with additional subjects such as modern, jazz, character [folk dances], and ballroom [social dances, such as the waltz, done with a partner]."

Lauren Anderson had other interests as a kid besides ballet, such as playing violin, skateboarding, rooting for Houston's sports teams, and playing Monopoly.

Lauren Anderson

BALLET DANCER
HOUSTON BALLET

Grew up in:
Houston, Texas
Age she started dance class: 7
Dance school: Houston Ballet Academy
Studied: Ballet, modern, jazz
Pets she had as a kid: Fish
Favorite books as a kid: *The Sweet Smell of Christmas;*
One Fish Two Fish Red Fish Blue Fish
Other activities as a kid: Violin, kickball, dodge ball,
volleyball, badminton, skateboarding, running,
watching pro sports, playing Monopoly
Class she takes now: Ballet
Other activities now: Pilates, computer games, singing, watching sports, playing with
her son, teaching master classes, giving Black History Month presentations
Music she listens to now to relax: Pop singers and jazz
Professional career: Houston Ballet; freelance ballet dancer

"I was always running and jumping as a kid. I wanted to run down the street faster than any boy," says Lauren Anderson. "My hand-eye coordination wasn't good, so baseball and basketball weren't my thing. But I was great at kickball and dodge ball. I loved to skateboard. I was very active." As her mother puts it, "Lauren was lively *all* the time."

Lauren's liveliness bubbled over even while she watched movie musicals on TV, including one she saw at about age five, *Singin' in the Rain.* "I remember there was a dancer in a green dress who was doing turns. I loved that," Lauren recalls. "I started doing it, too."

At age six, a different kind of turning thrilled her when she saw her first live ballet performance at a theater in Houston, where she grew up. "I don't remember what the ballet was, but I remember how I felt afterward. I felt great! I was flying. I loved ballet. I wanted to dance as much as I could." Clearly, it was time for dance classes.

Her parents asked around and found that the best ballet training was at the academy connected with the Houston Ballet company. From age seven until the end of high school, Lauren studied there after school, taking ballet and later adding some modern and jazz dance, too. After her first few months of ballet, seven-year-old Lauren was onstage as a ginger cookie in Houston Ballet's *The Nutcracker.*

SUGAR PLUM SIGHTINGS

Lauren was in *Nutcrackers* from age seven on; over the years, she did every female role except Clara and Clara's mom. She first danced the Sugar Plum Fairy at age nineteen.

Most of Houston Ballet's dancers were white, but that didn't keep Lauren from dancing nearly all the major female roles in classical ballet, including the one she's doing here: Cinderella, with Sean Kelly.

Her high energy level made her an enthusiastic learner but could also land her in hot water. "I got thrown out of class a lot because of my mouth, talking too much," she notes. Luckily, her teachers helped her get her spunky spirit in gear.

"WE *ARE* THE MUSIC"

"We always had music in the house. I can't remember not loving music," notes Lauren. Her mom was a music teacher; her father, a school principal, sang with church groups. In elementary school, Lauren started playing her mom's violin and kept at it all through middle school. "I loved violin. But when I needed private lessons, my parents said they couldn't afford to pay for lessons in both ballet and violin. They made me choose. I figured I could always go back to violin when I was sixty, but I couldn't still dance at sixty. So I chose ballet." She kept on with music by singing. "My friends and I would do our hair up with tinsel and pretend we were in girl groups like the Supremes."

The fun she had with music as a kid helped her as a dancer. "Music is the key. As dancers, we *are* the music. We express the feeling of the music. Music is something that has to be in you. Some of the best dancers may not be the best technically, but if they *are* the music, that's what makes it art."

"A HUGE GRIN"

Lauren's mom took her to lots of performances as a kid. One show stands out above all the rest, a performance by the Dance Theater of Harlem, a largely black ballet company that was visiting Houston. "My mom says I sat on the edge of my seat during the entire show with a huge grin on my face," recalls Lauren, who was nine years old then. At

---

CLASS-Y TIP

WHAT IT'S ALL ABOUT: "When I was a kid, I hated adagio," says Lauren. That's the part of class when students work on extension, seeing how high they can lift each leg and then hold it up in various positions. "I had bad legs, awful feet, and not much extension. Adagio was hard! It wasn't until I was older that I found ways to make it interesting and began to understand what it was all about: interpreting the music and making it look good." She tried to make each extension, no matter how high, look beautiful and capture the music's mood. "If only I knew that sooner. I wasted too many classes!"

Lauren is clearly following her own advice to "look like you're enjoying yourself" as she dances the role of Aurora in Sleeping Beauty.

that show, for the first time, Lauren saw an African American ballerina. "When a black girl in a tutu danced across the stage, I said, 'Mommy, look! She's black!' Then there was another. Then the whole stage was full of them. I couldn't believe it. The moment I saw that black ballerina, I knew that's what I wanted to be: a classical ballerina."

Before then, all the ballerinas she saw performing with Houston Ballet or with other companies that came to town were white. In ballet class, there was only one other black girl. When that girl dropped out, Lauren was the only black ballet student.

Her parents had thought dance would be just a hobby for Lauren, but when her father saw how serious she was becoming about it, he had a talk with her. "Because every other kid at the school was white, he said I had to be better than all those other kids if I wanted to get noticed. He said I had to always do my absolute best. But he wasn't putting any more pressure on me than I was putting on myself. I was already very competitive." For example, Lauren was a Monopoly fanatic and loved battling her way to victory in long marathon Monopoly games with her two best friends. She also enjoyed having friendly contests with another girl in ballet class. "If she did four turns, I had to do five. If I did five, she did six."

It was good that Lauren had such determination. She would need it to deal with some upsetting advice the head of Houston Ballet gave her.

CLASS-Y TIP

CROSS-TRAINING: Like Lauren, most dancers in this book cross-train, which means that in addition to dance, they exercise in other ways, doing such things as Pilates, yoga, or working out at a gym. For young students, it's best not to start heavy-duty cross-training too soon and to check with your teacher first. Houston Ballet's academy has students begin Pilates at about age twelve. The School of American Ballet in New York waits until age fourteen. Lauren never had a major injury during her long Houston Ballet career, something she feels was due to her solid ballet training and also to cross-training. "I had a couple of twisted ankles, but that was about it."

"A TRACK RUNNER'S BODY"

Ben Stevenson was the head of both Houston Ballet and its school back then. He liked Lauren's spirit. But because she didn't have the long, slender legs that many ballerinas have, he felt ballet might not be the best career for her. When she was thirteen, he told her that he saw a brighter future for her as a dancer in Broadway shows. "He said to keep taking ballet because it would be good for musical theater," says Lauren. "He wasn't mean about it. He didn't say I'd *never* get into the company. But I was upset. I wanted to be a classical ballerina!"

She didn't give up her dream. "I dug in and worked harder, taking ballet every day. I had a track runner's body, but I worked at shaping it to be more classical looking. I also began to understand that it's not just about good legs and feet and how high you get your legs. It's also about feeling the music. I started using my upper body and head more, to feel the music more."

Lauren also began to realize the importance of dancing with confidence, to make the most of what you *can* do. "If you take whatever you've got, make it in a nice line, interpret the music, do the choreography, and look like you're enjoying yourself, you're going to look good. How can you lose?"

Lauren made steady progress. At the end of high school, she made a deal with her dad. If she didn't find a dance job by a year after graduation, she'd go to college and try something else. Right after graduation, she enrolled in a summer course at Houston Ballet and worked really hard. At the end of the six-week program, Ben Stevenson was so impressed with her dancing that he offered eighteen-year-old Lauren a spot in Houston Ballet's corps de ballet. "I started jumping up and down, hugging and kissing everyone."

"STILL LEARNING"

While in the corps de ballet, Lauren kept polishing her skills and exploring ways to be a more expressive dancer. "I halfway understood what I had to do in my teens," she says. "But before I really got it, I was in my twenties. I'm still learning! I still take class every day." To keep slimming her thighs, she began to do Pilates exercises, which tend to strengthen and lengthen muscles without making them bulky.

After three years in the corps, she became a soloist. Four years later, she became a principal, one of the few African American principals in a major ballet company. By then Ben Stevenson was a big fan, as a result of Lauren's beautiful technique and also her talent for portraying the emotions of characters, from *Sleeping Beauty*'s gentle Aurora to *Swan Lake*'s sneaky Odile. He created a ballet for Lauren about Cleopatra, queen of ancient Egypt. In more than twenty years at Houston Ballet, Lauren danced nearly all the major female roles in classical ballet, along with quite a few modern roles. That's pretty amazing for a kid who once feared she had no future in ballet.

But all good things come to an end. In 2006, at age forty-one, Lauren left the company—not because she was ready to stop dancing, but because she wanted to dance even more! By then she was married to a jazz musician and was the mother of a lively toddler. However, she wasn't ready to hang up her pointe shoes. "In the company, I wasn't dancing as much as I used to," Lauren explains. The company had a new artistic director who didn't do as many of the classic story ballets that are Lauren's specialty. "I'm still in good shape and didn't want to sit around. I'd rather be dancing. It was time to become a freelance dancer and perform with other companies. I have dance gigs lined up for a couple of years."

Lauren is still involved with Houston Ballet, as its ambassador to young people. She speaks with students in schools to try to turn them on to dance and the arts. Working with kids is something she has been doing for years, teaching master classes and coaching young dancers in the Houston area. She has also kept up her interest in sports and for a while was a regular on a sports radio show, predicting football game winners. "It's important to have a life outside ballet. The more you experience, the more you bring to the stage. Ballet is art that comes from your soul."

Lauren with her son, Lawrence, who joined her at rehearsals shortly after he was born.

DANCE TALK   **MOMS DANCING**

In the early 1980s when Lauren first joined Houston Ballet, there weren't many ballerinas who were also moms. But by 2006, there were quite a few dancing moms in ballet companies. Besides Lauren, there were two other ballerinas at Houston Ballet who had young kids, as well as four dancing moms at New York City Ballet and five at American Ballet Theatre.

When Lauren was pregnant, she danced for the first five months of her pregnancy, including twirling about as the Sugar Plum Fairy. However, the extra weight from being pregnant made those turns feel "kind of weird." So right after *Nutcracker* season, this thirty-eight-year-old expectant mom took a few months off. However, shortly after her son was born, Lauren was back taking class and rehearsing, bringing the baby in his carrier. "It's great having a kid. It gives you new experiences to make your dancing more interesting," says Lauren.

The surfing John Selya did as a kid gave him an enthusiasm for "testing the limits" that he also brings to his dancing.

John Selya

FROM BREAKDANCING TO BALLET TO BROADWAY

Grew up in: New York, New York, and Atlantic City, New Jersey
Age he started dance class: 10
Dance schools: School of American Ballet;
LaGuardia High School of Music and Art and Performing Arts
Studied: Ballet, modern, breakdancing (on his own)
Pet he had as a kid: Dog named Peaches
Favorite books as a kid: Books about oceans and undersea explorers
Other activities as a kid: Surfing, soccer, baseball, running
Class he takes now: Ballet
Other activities now: Surfing, teaching dance
Music he listens to now to relax: All kinds
Professional career: ABT; Twyla Tharp Dance Company; *Movin' Out* and
The Times They Are A-Changin' (on Broadway); freelance dancer

"I was in the ocean, boogie boarding and surfing from a very young age," recalls John Selya. He grew up in New York City, but his family spent summers at the beach in Atlantic City, New Jersey. He loved getting in tune with the rhythm of the waves, paddling out into the ocean and waiting for just the right moment to balance on his surfboard and ride a wave toward shore.

At around age seven, he began getting in tune with another rhythm: the beat of disco music from the movie *Saturday Night Fever.* He was excited by the flashy dance routines John Travolta did in that film. "I'd put on the *Saturday Night Fever* recording and perform in the living room for my family, dancing like John Travolta."

Soon John added to his living room shows by doing the toy soldier's dance from *The Nutcracker.* His older sister studied ballet for a while at the School of American Ballet (SAB), which is connected to the New York City Ballet company. She got to be one of the kids in that company's *Nutcracker.* John visited her backstage and figured out how to do the toy soldier's dance. "I wanted to be part of *The Nutcracker,* too, but the only way to be part of it was to go to that school. So that's why I went." At age ten, he tried out for SAB's Children's Division, got in, and a year

SUGAR PLUM SIGHTINGS

John was in many *Nutcrackers* as a student at SAB. As an adult, he has been a guest *Nutcracker* soloist with a company in Hawaii, so he could hit the waves during his time off.

While in American Ballet Theatre's corps de ballet, John sometimes danced soloist roles. Here he's the pirate Birbanto in Le Corsaire, *with choreography by nineteenth-century choreographer Marius Petipa.*

later was a *Nutcracker* kid. "It was fun and it got me out of regular school early for rehearsals!"

"ALL THAT STUFF WAS FUN"

John took ballet at SAB on Saturday mornings and a few days a week after school. "Ballet class was not boring at all," he says. "We were jumping immediately. All that stuff was fun. I made great friends. We'd run around the halls and play before class." At first, boys and girls took class together. After about a year, he was in an all-boys class. "I had good friends at regular school, too. They didn't make fun of me for ballet. I was good at sports and played soccer and baseball. At that time, it was not uncommon for athletes to take dance to improve their skills."

Dance class not only helped his soccer footwork but also gave him a place to perform, besides his living room. Sometimes he did kids' roles for New York City Ballet and for another company in New York—American Ballet Theatre (ABT). In one ABT ballet, he danced with famous dancer Mikhail Baryshnikov. After a while, though, John grew tired of ballet. He wanted more time to hang out with friends. So at age

CLASS-Y TIP

HAVE FUN: One of John's teachers at SAB made class fun by encouraging students to go "full throttle" and try to jump higher and turn more, even if that meant making mistakes at first. "We'd cheer each other on," says John. Not only was it fun, but it helped them be more exciting dancers. "Keep the joy, no matter what, even if it means horsing around after rehearsal." Sometimes if ABT rehearsals grew boring, he'd lighten the mood during breaks with some breakdancing. To warm up before a performance, he revs himself up by listening to rap.

fourteen, he quit ballet. But he didn't quit dancing. He just changed the beat to hip-hop.

"YOU CAN LET LOOSE"

John's family moved to Atlantic City for two years while he was in junior high. He was thrilled to be living near the ocean year-round. Of course, he did a lot of surfing, but he also liked watching breakdancing movies with his Atlantic City friends. Breakdancing to hip-hop music was the cool new thing to do back then, in the early 1980s. He loved breakdancing's flips, spins, and the balancing on one hand or even one shoulder. "We taught ourselves how to do it. Then we'd do it on the boardwalk or at competitions in school gyms. It was fun."

After two years of this, John realized, "I missed ballet." His family was moving back to New York City. He decided to audition for SAB again. He was sixteen, and this tryout was for SAB's Advanced Division. It was a harder audition than the one he did six years earlier. Luckily, SAB accepted him, but only on probation: If he did well, he could stay; if he goofed off, he was out. "I was determined to be a dancer," he says. He stopped breakdancing and surfing for the time being. He spent his free time watching ballet videos of Mikhail Baryshnikov.

However, surfing and hip-hop had helped him. "Paddling into a big wave is scary. So is stepping onstage to dance. Surfing taught me to overcome fear and get joy from testing the limits." Breakdancing showed that "dancing doesn't have to be all uptight and proper. You can let loose." Breakdancing actually came in handy many years later in one of the most important jobs of his career.

"KIND OF A HEADSTRONG KID"

At SAB the second time around, John took ballet every day after high school and on Saturdays, too. "I was lucky to find friends at SAB who knew what it took to be disciplined and make progress, but who could still go out and have fun," he says. They had pirouette competitions after class and begged stars from New York City Ballet to share the secrets of doing amazing turns and leaps when those pros came to SAB for class. John even became a "flower boy," walking onstage after City Ballet performances to give ballerinas flowers. "That was awesome. I could stand in the wings and watch ballet all the time."

But there was one thing that wasn't fun: high school. He was at a school for young performers that let him take time off for dance classes. Even so, high school was not his thing. "When I started getting recognition from SAB teachers and realized I might be able to be a professional dancer, I quit high school and went to SAB full time. I was seventeen. I don't think my parents thought this was a good decision, but I was kind of a headstrong kid. I'm lucky they trusted me. I had a scholarship to SAB. I knew I could get a job if I finished the year strong."

He didn't try for a job with New York City Ballet. "I felt City Ballet liked tall dancers, and I wasn't tall," he notes. Instead, he auditioned for ABT, where Mikhail Baryshnikov was the artistic director. That audition went well, and at age eighteen John won a spot in ABT's corps de ballet. "I was in the corps for eleven years," he says. "At first it was great." Besides performing in New York, ABT tours a lot, doing shows in other cities. "The touring was fantastic. So were the friendships." When ABT was in California, sometimes on days off he'd go surfing. "I figured if I was dancing well, I could go surfing and shed some stress." In addition to his corps work, he did some solo roles with ABT and even choreographed a few ballets that ABT performed.

"Then it got to be less fun," he says. He wasn't promoted to be a permanent ABT soloist. He thought that might partly be because he was short and had a more muscular build than the typical tall, slender ballet dancer. He grew discouraged and left ABT. He thought about quitting dance altogether. But he didn't because soon he had a chance to combine his ballet skills with his love for (you guessed it) surfing and breakdancing.

"ANOTHER DIRECTION"

A year after leaving ABT, John had a call from Twyla Tharp, a choreographer who sometimes creates ballets for ABT. Her dances use a quirky blend of ballet and jazz, mixed with a loose-limbed, almost rubbery style of moving. She was forming her own company. Would John like to join? You bet! He had loved dancing in her ballets at ABT. In her new company, she worked with John and her other dancers to create new pieces. John's surfing inspired one piece: *Surfer on the River Styx*, in which he kicked and twisted his way through imaginary waves onstage. His breakdancing helped with another of her creations: *Movin' Out*, Twyla Tharp's prize-winning musical that played on Broadway in New York for three years.

Movin' Out is about a group of friends in the 1960s. The story is told completely by dance, with no words. John played a guy who serves in the Vietnam War, comes home shell-shocked, and searches for a way to make peace with himself. John used a lot of ballet in *Movin' Out*, but when his character's anger called for something stronger, he turned to breakdance. He would go from doing perfect ballet pirouettes in one scene to crashing to the floor in another scene and twirling upside down

---

INSIDE SCOOP
BEING IN A BROADWAY MUSICAL

GOOD POINTS: "You dance the same thing every night in a Broadway musical," says John. "That gives you a chance to really examine it and do something with it. In a ballet company, you might dance one particular ballet just five times during a season, if you're lucky. You can execute the steps in that ballet and be on the music, but you might not get so deeply into it."

BAD POINTS: "Dancing the same thing every night can be tiring," John adds. "You're using only certain muscles every night, so you need to take class to awaken those other muscles that you don't use in the show." Elizabeth Parkinson, who was also in *Movin' Out* and is featured later in this book, adds that Broadway is risky: "A show could close after a week and you have to look for the next job."

John's powerhouse performance in Movin' Out *won him several awards.*

on his shoulders. Or he'd charge up walls and do spiraling leaps in the air. This was a perfect role for his rugged, muscular body. He won awards for his explosive performance.

Doing *Movin' Out* night after night was tough, "both physically and mentally," John says. To keep his body ready for action, he took ballet class almost every day. "With Twyla's choreography, you use your ballet technique but take it in another direction." On days off, he'd relax by heading to beaches on nearby Long Island for some surfing. When the musical ended its run after three years, John took a long surfing vacation in Hawaii. Then it was back to New York to do some teaching and choreography, and to search for a new project that would use his special combination of dancing abilities. That search led him back to Broadway, where he danced once again in a Twyla Tharp musical: *The Times They Are A-Changin'.*

PERFORMANCE POINTER

PACE YOURSELF: *"Movin' Out* was hard, like being thrown to the lions every night," admits John. "From the moment I woke up until I did the show each night, I was in a constant state of preparation. I wouldn't walk around too much so I didn't get tired. I'd eat only bland food during the day so I wouldn't upset my stomach. I made sure to drink water because you don't want to realize fifteen minutes before you go on that you're dehydrated and then guzzle water and feel sick." Without enough water, muscles don't work right and tend to cramp. However, after a show, he would let loose and have fun—and all the spicy food he wanted.

DANCE TALK **WATCHING VIDEOS**

Studying videos of Mikhail Baryshnikov helped John get back on track with ballet after his two-year breakdancing time-out. "I immersed myself in those videos to see what needed to be done to be a good dancer," John explains.

Many dancers spent hours watching dance videos as kids. For Gillian Murphy, videos were the only way she saw professional dancers as a young girl. "I grew up in a pretty rural place and no big companies came through to perform," she says. "I never saw ABT live until I joined the company! But I saw ABT and other companies on videos. We also taped dance performances from TV. I'd watch a video of the Kirov Ballet's *Le Corsaire* before recitals to inspire me."

Your local library might have dance videos or DVDs to inspire you. Clifton Brown advises, "It's good to watch all kinds of videos, to have as much exposure as possible to different kinds of dance. It helps you become a better artist. You may not even know what you'd be best at if you haven't seen more of what's out there." (See resources, page 215, for viewing suggestions.)

Tess Reichlen in an outfit she wore to a dance competition. "I liked tap," she says, "but I haven't done it since I was thirteen."

Teresa Reichlen

BALLET DANCER
NEW YORK CITY BALLET

Grew up in: Clifton, Virginia

Age she started dance class: 3

Dance schools: Studios in northern Virginia, including Russell School of Ballet; School of American Ballet

Studied: Ballet, tap, jazz, modern, creative movement

Pets she had as a kid: Dogs named Bart, Ben, Nick, Sam, Calvin; cat named Daisy

Favorite books as a kid: The Goosebumps series

Other activities as a kid: Soccer, biking

Class she takes now: Ballet

Other activities now: Taking college courses, reading, watching baseball games, working out at a gym

Pets she has now: Cats named Mimi and Tony

Music she listens to now to relax: Classic rock, such as the Rolling Stones

Professional career: New York City Ballet

"I never went to soccer practice," says Tess Reichlen. But that didn't stop her from playing on soccer teams right up through eighth grade. "It was just understood that I could never come to practice because I had ballet after school." She didn't go to all her games either. She split her Saturdays: One Saturday she'd play soccer, and the next she'd go to dance class. "I liked playing soccer, even though people made fun of the way I'd go skipping down the field. Soccer was something to do besides dance. My best friend was on my team. After soccer we'd hang out, ride bikes, and play board games. I had a lot of soccer friends. They were my non-dance friends."

She also had dance friends. As she grew older, she spent more time with them. Tess had started dance at age three with creative movement classes at a studio near her Virginia home. Then she moved to other studios to take tap, jazz, and ballet. Tap and jazz were fun, but she liked ballet best. "I always loved ballet class. It was my favorite part of the day."

From fifth grade on, Tess took dance five or six days a week, doing mainly ballet but also some jazz and modern. "With my ballet friends, we'd be together three or four hours a day, taking class or rehearsing for performances. On weekends, we'd have sleepovers, watch ballet videos, make cookies, all that girl stuff." She also saw a lot of ballet performances in nearby Washington, D.C. "My parents took me whenever a big company was in town. I saw ABT and Alvin Ailey

Tess in a ballet Balanchine choreographed to Tchaikovsky's Piano Concerto Number 2.

American Dance Theater but not New York City Ballet. They didn't come to Washington."

At the start of high school, in ninth grade, she quit soccer to spend every Saturday dancing. "By then, all my friends were from ballet. I didn't have a social life at regular school. I did well in school but could never be in activities or go over to people's houses after school because I had ballet. I was kind of an outsider at high school. I felt bad not having high school friends. When you're in high school, you think it's the whole world, but when you leave, you realize it's not. I don't think I missed out on much." Soon Tess was busy mastering a new style of dance that let her become a real insider— in the world of ballet.

"NOT A NATURAL SHOW-OFF"

While growing up in Virginia, Tess switched dance studios several times. Each studio taught a slightly different style of ballet. So did the various summer programs she went to starting in fourth grade. These style changes didn't bother her. "It all came somewhat easily to me," Tess recalls. Even high leg lifts weren't a hassle. "I've always been very flexible."

But something else didn't come so easily: performing. "I liked performing, but I always got really nervous. I'm not a natural show-off kind of person," she

---

CLASS-Y TIP

JEALOUSY ALERT: "Girls I went to SAB with are my friends in the company," says Tess. "Sometimes you'll get angry if someone does better than you, but then you realize that's not something to be angry about. You have to leave it in the studio so you can still be friends."

says. Auditioning for summer programs made her nervous, too. Summer programs often hold tryouts in cities around the country, including Washington, D.C., where Tess auditioned. The auditions consist of taking a class that officials from the programs watch. "I would be nervous going in, but once I got into the class, I felt fine." The same with performing—once onstage, she'd do well.

One audition that was particularly stressful was for the summer program at the School of American Ballet (SAB), the school of New York City Ballet. "A few people from my dance school had auditioned for SAB, but nobody ever got in," says Tess. At fourteen, she gave it a try. During the audition, she watched nervously as SAB officials wrote down notes about her dancing. A few weeks later, she received a letter from SAB. She got in! "I was ecstatic," she says.

But she didn't go.

Tess knew SAB had high standards. The idea of going there was a little scary. "I thought I'd wait until I was older and more ready," she says. Plus, she hadn't won a scholarship. That summer she went to another program where she had a scholarship, the Rock School, part of Pennsylvania Ballet. She had been there before and liked it. The next year, Tess tried out again for SAB's summer course. She was accepted, won a

SUGAR PLUM SIGHTINGS

As a kid, Tess was in many *Nutcrackers* in Virginia, doing various roles, including Clara. With New York City Ballet, she has danced even more roles, from Dewdrop to the Sugar Plum Fairy.

scholarship, and this time was ready to face the challenge of learning to dance the SAB way.

"HOMESICK"

The style of ballet taught at SAB was developed by George Balanchine, one of the founders of New York City Ballet. "With Balanchine technique, things were different than I was used to in the way you hold your hands or cross your feet. You stand more forward," Tess explains. "It was hard to make the adjustments. It takes totally retraining your body." But SAB teachers were impressed with the progress she made that summer. They invited her to stay for the coming school year.

"I knew I couldn't improve anymore if I stayed at my old dance school in Virginia," notes Tess. So at age fifteen, she made the bold decision to keep studying at SAB. She lived in a dormitory with other SAB students and finished her last three years of high school at a special school in New York that's geared to kids who are training to be dancers, actors, and musicians. She wasn't an outsider at that school. Her new SAB friends went there, too.

PERFORMANCE POINTER

THE WHOLE PACKAGE: "I took a dance criticism class at college, and it helped so much," says Tess. In the class, students watched videos of different versions of the same ballet to figure out why they liked some performances more than others. "I didn't just love people with the best technique. I loved dancers who were great actors, who showed emotion and drew people in. I wish someone had pointed that out to me earlier because I didn't work on that as a girl. I was working on getting my legs right. You have to work on your upper body, too, on the acting part of performance, on getting your character into your dancing. It's the whole package that's important, not just turns and jumps."

"I was homesick the first year and phoned my parents a lot. They came to visit a lot, and I went home every three-day weekend. But I loved living in the dorm, being surrounded by other dancers. We were all young and homesick. We grew up together, became friends, and have stayed friends."

However, SAB classes were still a struggle. "It took the first half of the year to get the Balanchine technique, and almost the whole year before it became natural for me." She wasn't chosen for the school's *Nutcracker* that first year. "I was upset, but I understood it was because everything was so new for me. In a way, it was good because it made me work harder." That hard work paid off. The next year, at age sixteen, she became an apprentice with New York City Ballet, performing in its corps de ballet for *The Nutcracker* and other productions. The following year, she became an official corps member, performing nearly every night during the company's season while also finishing her senior year in high school. Often she had to skip her calculus class if she had rehearsals during the day. On Mondays, the company's day off, she would meet with her math teacher to go over any calculus she had missed.

"GIVE IT YOUR ALL"

"It's hard work being in the corps," explains Tess. "There's a lot of rehearsing, and you're dancing almost every night." Besides learning their corps parts, these dancers often understudy soloist roles and sometimes have to do those roles at the last minute if a soloist is injured. "The worst was when I was called at seven thirty on a night I wasn't dancing. I was in the dorm. They said I had to get to the theater right away to do *Symphony in C*. I had understudied the role and knew it pretty well. I ran across the plaza, rehearsed with the ballet mistress for an hour." A ballet mistress is a member of a dance company's staff who helps the dancers learn their parts. "Then I put on my makeup, went out, and did it. I enjoyed it, but it was nerve-wracking."

Tess was gradually feeling more at ease while performing. "It took being onstage a lot and watching other people onstage. I'd pick dancers I liked and take a close look at what they did, the difference in the effort they put into a performance as opposed to a rehearsal, the little things they did to heighten their performance. I learned that once you get out there, just give it your all, be self-confident and fearless. Don't worry about what people are going to think." Her growing confidence helped her shine in soloist roles she did while still in the corps. Her elegant dancing, with its hint of sassiness, combined

CLASS-Y TIP

TRY IT: "Teachers told me as a kid to do sit-ups, that everything is from the stomach. I never believed that until recently when I saw the difference when I finally started doing exercises to strengthen my core [stomach and abdominal muscles]," says Tess. "Having a strong core is essential to being able to go out onstage every night and trust that you can do something consistently. No matter how crazy it may sound, your teacher is usually right."

with her astonishing leg lifts, won her great reviews and a promotion. At age nineteen, Tess was promoted to the rank of official soloist with New York City Ballet.

"WHAT I ALWAYS WANTED TO DO"

At five feet nine inches, Tess is taller than many ballerinas and tends to do the "tall-girl" parts, or as she describes them, "flexible kick-your-leg parts," such as the fiery queen Hippolyta in *Midsummer Night's Dream* or the spunky lead in the "Rubies" section of *Jewels.* She has also done pieces that use some modern dance. "Modern is hard for me. I want to keep working at it. I'm still learning."

She is also doing another kind of learning as a science major at Barnard College, a school in New York that's not too far from the New York City Ballet theater. "I want to earn a college degree so I'll have a head start on doing something else once my dance career is over." But it will take a while to earn that degree. She usually has time for just one course a semester and can take only courses that meet from 9:00 to 9:50 in

INSIDE SCOOP
BEING A SOLOIST

GOOD POINTS: "Being a soloist is a different kind of dancing than being in the corps de ballet," explains Tess. "Soloist roles take more rehearsal. You have to think through the part more and put a lot more preparation into everything. The way you take the stage is different. You're out in front, there might be a spotlight on you, and you know people are applauding just for you. I like that. Who wouldn't?"

BAD POINTS: "There's more pressure, but the hardest part is there's no consistency in the schedule. You're not a principal, so you're not first in line to get a part." Some weeks, Tess might dance one role or none at all. The next week, she might be in several pieces. "It's feast or famine. I'm learning how to keep myself occupied and in shape when I'm not dancing a lot. I take class every day. If I don't have rehearsal, I'll work out at the gym."

Tess as the spunky lead dancer in the "Rubies" section of George Balanchine's ballet Jewels.

the morning—*before* her ballet day begins. She schedules her science lab work for her day off.

"It's good to have something else to think about besides dance so when I go home I don't just worry about every little detail in the show. If all your friends are dancers, you get so wrapped up in it that you forget how special it is. It can seem unglamorous when you're doing it: sweaty all day, exhausted, in pain sometimes. But when college friends say, 'Wow, that's the coolest job,' then I remember that it is cool to think that I'm actually doing what I always wanted to do."

 ## DANCE TALK **SUMMER FUN**

Like many dancers in this book, Tess went to summer dance programs as a kid. She learned a lot and had fun. Mikko Nissinen, artistic director of Boston Ballet, feels summer programs are good because "you get different kinds of teachers, a new environment, and can compare yourself to students your age from different parts of the country or the world. That enriches your understanding." Gillian Murphy agrees. What she liked about SAB's summer program was "being around other kids my age who were really talented. It inspired me. I also saw that my training may not have been as polished as some, but that I was doing well." Some programs require an audition. Others ask students to send in videotapes of their dancing. For a list of summer programs, check out dance magazines and their Web sites. (See resources, page 213.)

A teenaged Amar Ramasar practicing in a studio at the
School of American Ballet when he was in a program
designed to encourage boys to do ballet.

Amar Ramasar

BALLET DANCER
NEW YORK CITY BALLET

Grew up in: Bronx, New York
Age he started dance class: 11 (started ballet at age 14)
Dance schools: TADA! Theater Company; School of American Ballet;
LaGuardia High School of Music and Art and Performing Arts
Studied: Ballet, tap, jazz, modern
Pets he had as a kid: Cats named Molasses, Maria Elena, Elvis; dog named Bone
Favorite books as a kid: The Narnia, Lord of the Rings, and Harry Potter series
Other activities as a kid: Baseball, video games, debate team,
storytelling contests, being in musicals
Class he takes now: Ballet
Other activities now: Video games, reading, watching sports on TV,
working out at a gym, teaching dance
Music he listens to now to relax: All kinds
Professional career: New York City Ballet

"I was fourteen when I started ballet," says Amar Ramasar. "Fourteen is late to start, but I had a love for ballet, and that's what kept me going." He also had something else going for him: He loved to perform. He had done a lot of performing as a kid, just not in ballet. "I guess I was a natural performer. I never got nervous in front of a group of people."

His love of performing started in elementary school when he entered a storytelling contest—and won. This was a big deal in the Bronx section of New York City where he grew up. "You memorize a story and practice how to say it in front of people, how to make it exciting. I loved it!" He enjoyed being on his school's debate team, too. When he was eleven, a children's theater group—called TADA!—came to his school to audition kids to be in musical plays on weekends. They picked Amar. For the next three years, instead of playing ball with friends after school as he used to, Amar took a long subway ride downtown every afternoon to rehearse. He had so much fun that he started doing plays in school, too.

TADA! gave kids classes in jazz and tap. That's when Amar discovered he loved to dance. His Puerto Rican grandmother already knew that, from watching Amar, at age five, bouncing to the beat when she put on salsa music. "She always said I was going to be a dancer,"

SUGAR PLUM SIGHTINGS

Amar wasn't in *The Nutcracker* as a kid. He did his first as a New York City Ballet apprentice and has since done hundreds more, dancing such roles as Mouse King, Cavalier, and a hilarious Mother Ginger.

Amar remembers. There was lots of music at his house, from salsa to jazz to the Hindu songs sung by his dad's father, who came from Trinidad.

Amar's uncle also saw dance in Amar's future. This uncle, Daniel Catanach, had been both a ballet and a modern dancer, and lived in Europe for many years. When Amar was fourteen, his uncle moved to New York, and Amar met him for the first time. "My uncle showed me dance videos and thought I could be a dancer. He said I should do ballet." Not only that, his uncle wanted Amar to aim high and audition for the School of American Ballet (SAB) at New York City Ballet. But without any ballet training, what chance did Amar have to get into SAB?

"VERY LUCKY"

No surprise: Amar didn't get into SAB's summer program when he first auditioned at age fourteen. But his uncle had sparked Amar's curiosity, and that summer Amar took ballet at a program run by American Ballet Theatre. In the fall, he auditioned again for SAB, which had recently started a new program to encourage boys to study ballet. The teacher of this program, Olga Kostritzky,

INSIDE SCOOP
BEING IN THE CORPS DE BALLET

GOOD POINTS: "Guys in the corps are very supportive of each other," says Amar. "We want everyone to succeed. If one corps guy gets to do a soloist part, we'll watch and let him know what he could do better. It's constructive criticism. Then we'll go upstairs and play video games." Yes, New York City Ballet has a room where dancers unwind with video games!

BAD POINTS: "Being in the corps is a lot of work. Of course, principals have harder stuff to do. But while I was in the corps, sometimes I did a principal part in the first ballet, a soloist in the next, and then the corps, all on the same night. It takes a lot out of you."

decided that even though Amar didn't know much ballet, he had the potential to become a great dancer. He was accepted. "I was very lucky," says Amar.

By then, he was going to a special arts high school across the street from SAB. Amar was thrilled to be at a high school where he could make up for lost time in dance by taking ballet and modern during the school day, along with regular academic courses. After school each day, first he did his homework and then headed across the street to SAB.

"I liked the challenge. I always wanted to learn more," says Amar. He was also learning a lot from his uncle, who had started his own company, Urban Ballet Theater, which does a mix of ballet, modern, and jazz. "During time off from SAB, I would dance with my uncle's company. I did so many types of dance with him. I would go over to his house and we would watch ballet videos for hours."

What did Amar's friends in his Bronx neighborhood think of his dancing? "I got teased, but it wasn't bad. They'd go, 'You have to wear *tights?*' And I'd say, 'Yeah, but I'm surrounded by beautiful women!' Everyone was cool. I played ball with them and was good at sports. I was a big Yankees fan. Still am. That helped a lot."

"WATCHING THE GREATS"

However, Amar soon grew frustrated with juggling two sets of ballet classes, those at high school and those at SAB. "The high school teachers would tell me to do things one way. SAB would try to get me to do something different. There were differences in timing and how you work at things. SAB is about making long lines, having fast and precise footwork. The way you move your arms at SAB is so different, making them not look restricted or stiff. I enjoyed SAB more. It gives you more free movement." So in eleventh grade, at age sixteen, Amar took a five-hour test, called the GED (General Educational Development). If he passed the test, he would earn a certificate that was the same as having a high school diploma. He passed. Then he quit high school to go to SAB full-time. "I was so happy! I moved into the dorm, which was like a big family."

Even though he was now learning only one style of ballet, it was still hard. "There were plenty of times I was totally discouraged. I wasn't born with great feet. My feet are big, flat, and don't point easily. I had to work on that, and on my turnout. I had difficulty with pirouettes and double tours. I would look around and see people in class who could do all this stuff. If only I had started even two years earlier, it would have come easier. I just had to work harder. I've gotten better, but I'm

PERFORMANCE POINTER

SMILE: "As an apprentice, I was thrown into so many ballets at the last minute," says Amar. He learned the choreography in a hurry, working in a rehearsal room as a pianist played the music and the ballet mistress taught him the steps. Even so, at times he was shaky on the choreography when he went onstage. "Sometimes there's a lot of whispering onstage with people trying to help, saying, 'Go over here. Follow me.' I figure if I smile, nobody will know the difference." What if he makes a blooper? "I laugh it off. There's no point dwelling on it. It happens to everybody."

always going to be working on those things. If I had a bad day at SAB, I would watch a ballet that night and that would lift me up. SAB gave us free tickets to New York City Ballet. I went to every show I could. I felt I could learn from watching the greats."

"DEAL WITH IT"

Amar kept training in the summer, too. "Olga said if I wanted to dance with New York City Ballet one day, I had to go where its dancers were and make that my focus." So he took class from Olga at a summer program in Saratoga Springs, New York, where the company performs in the summer. After finishing there, he headed to Philadelphia for the Rock School's summer program, where Olga also taught.

"Olga was like a drill sergeant. She made us take off leg warmers, look in the mirror, deal with it, not hide the problem. I hated barre, standing there looking in the mirror. But barre really breaks things down. The repetition is so important. Some people find Olga kind of blunt and can't take it, but I loved it. She was like gold for me. She didn't tiptoe around me, but made me work harder. She gave corrections in a good way that made you really want to do better. The more I wanted it, the better I got."

He not only improved but had fun, too. "We'd have pirouette contests, or see what tricks we could do. If you have a love for it and keep it happy, that helps you through the hard times." The sparkling enthusiasm of

Amar in a New York City Ballet piece choreographed by Jerome Robbins, Concertino, *set to music by Igor Stravinsky.*

his performances in workshop productions at SAB helped him win an invitation to become an apprentice with New York City Ballet at age eighteen, just four years after he started ballet.

Apprentices can take company class with New York City Ballet's regular dancers. "At my first company class, I couldn't concentrate. I was back in the corner, in awe of the famous dancers in the room, seeing them do these incredible things. Finally, I said to myself, 'Amar, you're here for a reason. You should be dancing, too.' Now I like company class. I try to go every morning. It starts the day in a good way."

"NOTHING COMPARES"

At New York City Ballet, apprentices have to perform in nine ballets before they can become full, official members of the corps de ballet. "I was cast in the corps in two ballets, but most of the seven others I got literally the day before. One time a guy sprained his ankle and I learned his part during intermission. I'm a quick learner," Amar recalls. To learn parts in a hurry, he would work in a rehearsal room with the ballet mistress. "Going to the ballet every night as a student at SAB helped. I have a photographic memory. I can see a ballet and it will stay with me. Taking tap, jazz, and modern as a kid helped,

TRAINING TIP

FEET UP: "Of course, you have pain. Pain is your life, but that's not going to stop me. There's physical therapy here and I go for any little thing or for a massage for tight muscles," says Amar. After a performance, he might put ice on sore muscles, or heat, whatever the therapist recommends. "When I'm home watching TV, I put my feet up."

Amar's enthusiasm for dance comes through loud and clear in this New York City Ballet production of Jerome Robbins's jazzy ballet, Fancy Free, *set to music by Leonard Bernstein.*

too. Some contemporary ballets have jazz-related steps, so knowing jazz helps." After a year as an apprentice, Amar became a full member of the corps. Besides doing corps parts, he also did some soloist roles. Four years later, he was promoted and became an official soloist.

"Dancing is still a challenge," notes Amar. "It doesn't get easier, but it keeps me happy, keeps me wanting more, wanting a taste of something new. When I know I have something hard coming up, I'll go every day to the gym and do the bike or the elliptical trainer, to try to get the stamina up. Some of these ballets can be a killer. But onstage, I love it. When I step onstage to do a *Nutcracker* pas de deux, at first I might get a little pinch in my stomach, but then I look at the audience, and there's that wonderful music and the ballerina, and it's incredible. It really is. Nothing compares."

DANCE TALK   **LATE STARTERS**

Amar had an advantage that helped him succeed in ballet despite a late start: He was a boy, and so he didn't have to dance on pointe. "I've never seen girls become professional ballet dancers if they haven't danced at all by fourteen," says Kay Mazzo, co-chairman of the faculty at the School of American Ballet. "It has to do with learning how to use your feet when you go on pointe. It takes years to do that. Ballet is unforgiving in what it demands of your body." In addition to pointe problems, she explains that "if your hips aren't loose and you don't have turnout, you probably won't be a professional ballet dancer."

However, some ballerinas, such as ABT's Carmen Corella, began at age thirteen, just before Kay Mazzo's cutoff. So did Elizabeth Parkinson, a dancer you'll meet later in the book. Shelly Power of Houston Ballet's academy adds, "We like girls and boys to start ballet as early as seven but at least by age ten." She points out that some boys tend not to get serious about ballet until later, including Houston Ballet's own current artistic director, Stanton Welch. He didn't start ballet until he was seventeen. However, in other kinds of dance a late start isn't such a problem. Late-starters—male and female—have done well in modern dance, Broadway shows, and in music videos, too.

Lauren Grant at one of her first recitals.

Lauren Grant

MODERN DANCER
MARK MORRIS DANCE GROUP

Grew up in: Highland Park, Illinois
Age she started dance class: 3
Dance schools: Local studios in Highland Park and Skokie, Illinois;
Chicago City Ballet School; New York University's Tisch School of the Arts
(earned a Bachelor of Fine Arts degree)
Studied: Ballet, modern, jazz, flamenco, character dance
Pets she had as a kid: Goldfish
Favorite books as a kid: Grimms' fairy tales;
The Lion, the Witch, and the Wardrobe
Other activities as a kid: Skiing, ice skating, gymnastics,
piano, acting, choreography
Class she takes now: Ballet
Other activities now: Gardening, baking, Pilates, working out at a gym,
teaching dance, going to concerts, plays, and museums
Music she listens to now to relax: Classical and jazz
Professional career: Mark Morris Dance Group (before that: freelance dancer)

Lauren Grant has had her ups and downs with *The Nutcracker*. As a kid, she was heartbroken when she wasn't cast in a big *Nutcracker* production in Chicago, one that she and other Chicago-area students were dying to be in. It wasn't just that she was turned down after auditioning during middle school. What was so upsetting was what the audition officials *said*. "They said my dancing was good enough, but my *look* wasn't right," Lauren recalls. "I had the wrong body type. I didn't have the tall, slender ballerina look. I was very short. Still am. I have a muscular lower body. I felt horrible! I wanted to be a ballerina. After they said that, I knew it probably wasn't going to happen."

However, that put-down actually helped her, by spurring her to find her true path in dance, one that led years later to a job with a top company by being cast—believe it or not—in a nutty *Nutcracker*.

Lauren had started dancing at age three, when her parents enrolled her in creative movement classes so she would have something to keep her busy while her dad was at work and her mom started law school. Lauren liked the classes and was soon taking ballet at a

---

PERFORMANCE POINTER

FUEL UP: As a teen, Lauren was Aurora in her ballet school's production of *Sleeping Beauty*. "I practiced all year for that one performance. I did it great in the studio. But I was nervous on the day of the performance and didn't eat enough. I had only one bowl of cereal all day." The performance went well until the end of the Rose Adagio, when she had to stand on one foot—on pointe—as a man took her hand to turn her around. "I got weak and fell off pointe and could not get back on. It was so sad. If I had eaten better, I would have had a reserve of energy. Now I have a big breakfast on performance day and then a light lunch."

Lauren in a powerful performance in Mark Morris's Gloria, *set to music by Antonio Vivaldi.*

studio upstairs from a T-shirt store in the Chicago sub-
urb where she lived. At this studio, she learned a Russian style of ballet that stressed powerful dancing. "I
loved it, especially the jumping." She
also loved going into Chicago to see
performances by American Ballet Theatre and other visiting companies. By
age eight, she was taking class at the
Chicago City Ballet School, run by
Maria Tallchief, a former New York
City Ballet dancer. But Lauren didn't
like this school's Balanchine style, with

SUGAR PLUM SIGHTINGS

Lauren is one of the four
dancers in this book who wasn't
a *Nutcracker* kid.

its emphasis on tall, long-legged, willowy dancers. So at age twelve, she switched to a school in the nearby town of Skokie, where she studied the Russian style she liked better. "I took class there every day. Everybody took turns driving me: my parents, grandparents, and my older brother and sister. They were so happy when I turned sixteen and could drive myself."

"HANDLING THIS"

Lauren dabbled in other activities as a kid: piano lessons, ice skating, skiing, and gymnastics. "Ballet was the winner. There's an emotional element in dance that's not there in gymnastics. I loved dancing to music and the connection with the audience of being onstage in a theater that is charged with energy. The dance school in Skokie put on ballets every year in a big community theater. It felt very professional."

She also enjoyed "the challenge of picking up different combinations in class. We'd learn a combination and then my teacher would say, 'Now reverse it and do it on the other side.' It's like doing a puzzle, very stimulating for the brain. You get amazing discipline from dance." That discipline carried over to schoolwork. "My parents were concerned about me taking so much dance, but my grades were good and so they thought, 'Okay, she's handling this.'"

However, handling that *Nutcracker* disappointment in middle school wasn't easy. Also hard to take was the advice a Chicago dance teacher dished out a few years later. "He told me, 'Don't bother. Just quit.' I didn't listen to him. But I struggled with feeling that maybe I wasn't skinny enough. I never had anorexia, but I battled with those feelings." She talked things over a lot with her mom. "Luckily, we both had good heads on our shoulders. I had strength of character and stayed true to myself." As for those powerful thighs that helped her be such a super jumper, she stopped fretting about them. "That's just the way I was built. I let my love of dance take over." It was leading her in new directions.

"WHOLE OTHER WORLD"

"A classmate at ballet school gave me a book to read," says Lauren. "She was older and was going to college, where she studied modern dance." The book was *Private Domain* by Paul Taylor, a famous choreographer who had his own modern dance company. In the book, he says that he always likes to have a short female dancer in his company. "My friend helped open my mind to modern dance." Maybe that's where Lauren would find her place in the world of dance.

In high school, Lauren signed up to take modern dance, which was part of the school's physical education program. "It was so exciting to see that there was

JITTERS BUSTER

PICTURE IT: "Having the jitters before a performance is normal," says Lauren. "Jitters get you exhilarated, and that helps you do better. But jitters can make you feel weak in the knees." To keep nerves under control, Lauren recommends using visualization, a strategy athletes use, too. "Picture in your mind what you're about to do and imagine doing it well. That calms you down and gets you focused. So does deep breathing."

INSIDE SCOOP
BEING IN A MODERN DANCE COMPANY

GOOD POINTS: Mark Morris's company is one of the few modern dance groups that always has real musicians play during performances. "It's great to dance to live music. Everything we do is choreographed by Mark. To originate a part and watch him work is exciting. His range is vast," says Lauren. David Leventhal adds: "There are no principals in the company. Everybody has a lot of group dancing to do and then a few special solos."

BAD POINTS: The company tours a lot, and that's hard. Lauren adds, "Mark is demanding. You're not going to be praised every day. Just being in the company is praise enough. You need to be able to take criticism and still love yourself."

this whole other world out there. From ballet, I thought the only thing you do with your foot in dance was point it and lift it. But in modern dance, you can flex it, relax it, bend it. You can drop your head. You can be on the floor and roll around. I never thought of these possibilities before. My high school put on a big dance show every year. I always choreographed a piece or two. I was also in school plays, acting and directing. It was a great time for me. I felt very creative."

She still took ballet, just not every day because she had rehearsals for her high school shows. The summer after tenth grade, she even did a summer ballet program at Boston Ballet. "But I realized I just wasn't quite the right type." The next summer, she switched to modern dance, taking a course in modern at New York University (NYU). While in New York City, she found out where Paul Taylor's studio was and took a class there. "It was thrilling! I decided to go to NYU for college." She applied, was accepted, and after her high school graduation, headed off to study modern dance at NYU's Tisch School of the Arts.

"FREELANCE DANCER"

In her early days at NYU, Lauren still had a lot of the straight-back ballerina in her. "I had to free myself from that and learn to let go, to release, to have more mobility. It was hard. But when I got that, it felt wonderful. It was so freeing, a whole new way of moving." She also did Pilates and kept taking ballet, too. "The ability to do both ballet and modern meant I was ready for anything."

She made good contacts at college. "We did so many performances. Choreographers came to them. When I

TYPICAL DAY

Lauren's typical rehearsal day starts with company class (ballet) in the morning, followed by several hours of rehearsals. About twice a week, she does Pilates before company class. On some days, she teaches a modern class in the evening at the Mark Morris Dance Center's school. When on tour, the workday can be very long. After arriving at a new theater to perform, the first day's rehearsal might last "from ten in the morning until eleven at night," notes Lauren. They have to rehearse with the local orchestra and see how their dances work in the new space. Long hours are also the rule on days with both afternoon and evening shows. "Sometimes I'll see the sky outside for only a few seconds," says Lauren. To keep her energy up and muscles from cramping, she drinks water and stretches a lot. "Stretching is a muscle-saver, but it's important to stretch properly." (Ask your teacher.) "At the end of a long day, I try to have a nice, satisfying dinner, although it may be nearly midnight. Then I'll take a hot bath and rub down my legs with oil."

The intensity that Lauren brings to her performances makes her fascinating to watch, as in this scene from Mark Morris's Mozart Dances.

graduated, I had offers to be in some shows. Not with anyone major, but it was nice to go right into rehearsals. I became a freelance dancer, going to auditions, being in a show here, a show there." She was good at learning quickly the choreography she was taught at auditions. "I have this ability to see a combination once and then do it. Part of that may come from the training I had growing up of having to reverse a combination in ballet class immediately, without thinking about it."

Six months after graduation, she got her big break. The Mark Morris Dance Group, one of the top modern dance companies, needed extras for Mark Morris's *The Hard Nut,* a comic version of *The Nutcracker.* The company asked NYU to suggest some dancers. NYU suggested Lauren.

It didn't bother Mark Morris that Lauren was short. His dancers range from tall to short, and from slim to curvy. His pieces use both ballet and modern, combined with exuberant, foot-stomping folk dances. He has a knack for bringing music to life in ways that are unexpected and often quite funny. Lauren fit right in, being both a graceful dancer and a spunky one, with a good sense of humor. "I got the job,"

CLASS-Y TIP

YOU NEVER KNOW: In her ballet training, Lauren took "character" dance classes in which she learned folk dances that are sometimes used in classical ballets. At about age eleven, Lauren was at a summer ballet camp where she learned the Spanish flamenco and had fun doing its dramatic foot stamping while clicking castanets with her fingers. Those skills came in handy later when she was in Mark Morris's company and he was creating a new piece in which he wanted to do flamenco dancing with another dancer. "At rehearsal Mark asked, 'Who can play the castanets?' I was the only one! I got to do the duet with him," says Lauren. "It's called *From Old Seville.* It's very funny."

she says. "I was a snowflake and a flower. It was only two weeks of work, but they liked me."

"JUMPING FOR JOY"

A few months later, Mark Morris again needed extra dancers for a big new piece he was creating. "They remembered me and asked if I'd be in it. I was jumping for joy! It was amazing to be in something while he was choreographing it." For about a year, she kept being hired as an extra, until finally she was invited to join the Mark Morris Dance Group. She was twenty-three years old.

"My acting training in high school has helped because there's a lot of acting in Mark's dances," Lauren explains. Her strong ballet background has helped, too, not only with the dancing but also in becoming a backup teacher for company class. "We always have a ballet class a few hours before a performance. Mark usually teaches it, but when he's not around, I teach it. Ballet is a good foundation for us. We do a lot of steps that require ballet training." She also teaches in the school the company has at its headquarters in Brooklyn. "I teach everything, from little kids' classes to adult beginners. When we're on tour, I lead master classes at universities. I think my next thing might be teaching."

Another dancer was hired as an extra around the same time as Lauren: David Leventhal (featured in the next chapter). "We became friends and would hang out," recalls Lauren. "Then we fell in love." Seven years after joining the company, they married. Guess which show they are featured in each holiday season? *The Hard Nut.* David is the Nutcracker who turns into a prince and falls in love with Lauren's character. "It's great to dance together," says David. "Especially," Lauren adds, "when you can fall in love onstage."

DANCE TALK   LOOKIN' GOOD

Like several other pros in this book, Lauren proves that a dancer doesn't have to be tall and stick-thin to succeed. Her story also shows that coming to terms with your body type can be tough at times. Shelly Power of Houston Ballet's academy notes, "When students go through puberty, their bodies change tremendously. Weight distribution is constantly fluctuating. We guide dancers through this difficult time with help from professionals. Nutritionists and doctors will look at a student's body mass index [a relationship between height, weight, and body fat] rather than looking only at weight. Dancers need to be lean but also healthy, and stay within safe levels determined by professionals. They need to be able to say, 'This is the body I've been given. I'm going to take care of my body.' Then together, the school's director and the student will figure out the right artistic path for the student. If students respect their bodies, they will dance longer and healthier with less chance for injury."

Kay Mazzo of the School of American Ballet adds, "There aren't many who go overboard, but we watch carefully. If someone is too thin in an audition, we won't accept them. If a student comes here and starts getting too thin, we talk with the parents and get them to a doctor and nutritionist." Lauren's advice: "Be healthy, let your body be what it was meant to be, and try your hardest at what you love to do. If you let that love come through, you'll find your place in life. Every *body* is beautiful."

David Leventhal's ballet training helped him in soccer.
"With ballet, your footwork is so precise," he says.

David Leventhal

MODERN DANCER
MARK MORRIS DANCE GROUP

Grew up in: Newton, Massachusetts

Age he started dance class: 8

Dance schools: Boston Ballet School; Green Street Studios; Brown University (earned a Bachelor of Arts degree)

Studied: Ballet, modern

Pets he had as a kid: Hamsters named Vladimir, Hannibal, Roger

Favorite books as a kid: *The Lion, the Witch, and the Wardrobe; Charlotte's Web, Stuart Little; James and the Giant Peach*

Other activities as a kid: Ice skating, piano, soccer, school plays, editor of high school newspaper

Class he takes now: Ballet

Other activities now: Cooking, playing piano, working out at a gym, teaching dance, helping to manage his apartment building, going to concerts, plays, and museums

Music he listens to now to relax: Classical and jazz

Professional career: Mark Morris Dance Group (before that: freelance dancer)

Ice skaters turned David Leventhal on to dance. When he was seven or eight years old, he loved to watch figure skaters on TV as they danced on the ice, doing amazing spins and jumps to beautiful music. He already knew how to skate. He couldn't wait to start dancing on the ice, too. But that wasn't so easy.

"What I wanted to do was so much more advanced than what I could do on the ice at my level," David recalls. Skaters have to put in a long time mastering the basics before they can spin or jump. "That's true in ballet as well, but in ballet you can try stuff out and fall, and it's no big deal. It's more difficult to do turns and jumps on a very thin blade. If you fall on the ice, it's very painful and very cold!"

Skating had another drawback, besides painful spills on the ice. Other boys in his Massachusetts town played ice hockey. "My father thought hockey was kind of dangerous for me because I was on the small side. So I took figure-skating lessons. I was the only boy in the class, with twenty girls. It felt strange, but that isn't why I stopped skating. I stopped because it was frustrating. I wanted to jump and turn like the skaters on TV. I had this bug inside me that made me want to dance."

Soon he found a warmer place to twirl and jump to beautiful music: at a class for boys at Boston Ballet School. A friend had signed up, and eight-year-old David joined him. "There were about six other boys in the class. It was a mix of pre-ballet and creative movement, taught by a male dancer from Boston Ballet. I loved it. I was small and scrawny for my age, but the thrill of being able to move to music and feel the power of that was very exciting." The next year, David moved on to a real ballet class. Before long, he was in Boston Ballet's *Nutcracker.* He kept at it for five years, until burnout got the better of him.

"NEEDED A BREAK"

Ballet was only one of David's activities as a kid. He also played soccer on Saturdays. "I liked the team part of soccer and that it was outside. I was fast, and I was confident when I had the ball. But I was always a little timid in sports and tried to get rid of the ball quickly so kids wouldn't charge at me."

He took piano lessons, too. They didn't work out very well. "I was very musical, but piano was difficult for me. I could pick up melodies and play them, but I wouldn't practice. It was slow going." He kept plugging away at piano lessons until the end of junior high because he loved music. So did his parents: His mom played flute and taught music; his dad sang in a community chorus. David wanted a way to express himself through music. He found it in dance.

"Dance came more easily to me," he explains. He was onstage a lot, dancing to beautiful music, not only in *The*

SUGAR PLUM SIGHTINGS

David started as a party kid in Boston Ballet's *Nutcracker* and then was Fritz for several years. In college, he was in the José Mateo Ballet Theatre's *Nutcracker* in Boston.

David dancing with his wife, Lauren Grant, in The Hard Nut, *Mark Morris's humorous version of* The Nutcracker.

Nutcracker, but also in Boston Ballet's *Sleeping Beauty* and *Romeo and Juliet.* "One year with *The Nutcracker,* I did thirty-two shows, dancing almost every night all December. I'd bring homework to the theater." By age twelve, he was taking ballet six days a week. "It was great, but it was also exhausting. I was getting burned out. I started not enjoying it anymore. I needed a break. When I was thirteen, I quit."

"NOT AS INTENSELY AS BEFORE"

David may have quit ballet class, but he kept dancing on his own. "I would put on music at home and dance in the living room, just for fun," he says. He also acted in musicals at his junior high school. When the holidays rolled around, he went to see Boston Ballet's *Nutcracker.* "It was hard sitting there in the theater, watching dancers I knew. I wasn't sure I had made the right decision."

After junior high, David and his family spent a year in England because his father, a professor, was working there. At the end of that year, David had a chance to do a two-week summer ballet program at London's Royal Academy of Dance. He gave it a try. "Not having danced for two years, I was a little shaky. But it was great! I decided to dance again, just not as intensely as before."

Back home in Massachusetts, he took class at Boston Ballet again—but only once or twice a week. He wasn't in the pre-professional part of the school anymore. He took classes for kids who dance just for fun. He didn't perform in *Nutcracker*s or anything else. He was too busy being the editor of his high school newspaper. He thought he might become a professional writer someday. After high school, he went to Brown University in Providence, Rhode Island, and majored in English literature. Then he discovered modern dance.

"GETTING WORK AND GETTING PAID"

Brown University offered modern dance classes, but no ballet. "My first month at Brown, I tried a modern class. It was really fun," says David. "It was more personal and expressive for me than ballet. I started taking as many classes as I could." He started performing with the university's modern dance group. But dance was just a hobby for him, until the summer after his sophomore year.

That summer he took a modern dance workshop at the Jacob's Pillow dance festival in Massachusetts, studying with teachers who used to be in Paul Taylor's modern dance company. They taught David some Paul Taylor choreography, with its high-spirited way of taking ordinary actions—running, walking, skipping, or even tumbling—and turning them into dance. David

---

TYPICAL DAY

Here's David's schedule for a day right before the Mark Morris company went on tour to Austria.

8:15 A.M. — Exercise in his apartment building's gym for thirty minutes

10:45 A.M. — Do Pilates at the Mark Morris Dance Center studio

11:00 A.M. — Company ballet class

12:45 P.M. — Work with Mark Morris on a new dance he's creating

2:00 P.M. — Co-teach a movement class for people with Parkinson's disease

2:45 P.M. — Lunch

3:00 P.M. — Rehearse pieces to be performed in Austria

6:00 P.M. — Speak with a reporter about what it's like to be a dancer

6:30 P.M. — Shower at the studio

7:15 P.M. — Go home to cook dinner (David loves to cook!)

---

loved his summer there. "Those three incredible weeks at the Pillow made me decide to consider dance as a career."

Back at college that fall, David got a call from someone in Boston who knew him from his Boston Ballet days. She asked if he could fill in for a dancer who broke his leg and couldn't do a *Nutcracker* that was about to open, not at Boston Ballet but at another Boston company. It wasn't a huge dancing part, and Boston was only an hour's drive away. So David did it. Then other Boston dance groups—both ballet and modern—began asking him to perform. "I was getting work and getting paid! This passion I'd had for dance for so long was starting to seem like a career possibility," David says. "Maybe I could really do this." His last two years at college were busy: He kept taking English literature courses while also going to Boston a few times a week to rehearse, perform, or take class at a studio in nearby Cambridge. After graduating, he went home and worked in a restaurant for six months to earn money. Then he made the big move to New York City to try to find work as a dancer.

AUDITION ADVICE

CHILL: David was two hours late for the biggest audition of his career, the one for being an extra in the Mark Morris company. It was a two-day audition: On the first day, dancers learned the steps; on the second day, they did the steps for Mark Morris. But David had a rehearsal for a freelance dance job during the same time as the first day's audition. He went to the rehearsal and then rushed to the audition, getting there right before it ended. "I learned as much of the dance as I could in the few minutes I was there," he says. "When I went back the next day, I had so little hope of getting the job that I was totally relaxed. I was more relaxed than for other auditions. I thought I'd do it for fun, because the movement was so much fun and the music was so great." Surprise! He got the job. The secret of his success: Relax and try to have fun.

"NOTHING BETTER"

"The first months in New York were difficult," David admits. "I didn't know anyone in the dance scene, but I had recommendations of where to take class." Taking class was a great way to find work. A teacher of one class had a small dance company and gave David one of his first jobs. The teacher needed to replace an injured dancer, remembered David from class, and asked him to fill in. Soon David was working as a freelance dancer with other people he met in class.

He got the most important audition of his career thanks again to someone he met in a class. A dancer in the Mark Morris Dance Group remembered David from a class they both used to take back in Boston and suggested David when Mark Morris needed extra dancers for an upcoming tour. David loved Mark Morris's dances because so many were set to David's favorite kinds of classical music. He did a great job at the audition and got the job. For about a year he kept being hired as a Mark Morris extra, until at age twenty-four he was invited to join the company, around the same time as Lauren Grant, later to be his wife.

David likes the variety of kinds of pieces the company performs, "the

SURVIVAL STRATEGY

TEMP WORK: Freelance dance jobs, especially in modern dance companies, often don't pay much, if anything. It helps to have a survival job. Some freelancers teach Pilates or work in restaurants. David signed up with a temp agency, which finds people temporary work in offices, doing such things as answering phones or typing. "Temp work is flexible," David says. "I could tell the agency I had an audition and couldn't work the next day." No problem. The agency would send another person to do the office job.

David as a bird in one of Mark Morris's most famous pieces, L'Allegro, il Penseroso ed il Moderato, *set to music by George Frideric Handel, the kind of glorious classical music David loves.*

range of moods, movement styles, and music. Mark isn't interested in pushing the body to do things it wasn't designed to do. He's more interested in creating shapes with groups of people than in daredevil acrobatics." But David adds that working with Mark while he's creating a new piece can be tricky. "You have to be able to learn new movement quickly, trying to keep up with Mark's mind, to show him what he's making up so he has a sense of the dance, while also trying not to get on his nerves."

Like Lauren, David teaches in the company's school. He still plays piano and thinks he might become a writer someday. But nothing could be as much fun for him as dance. "I'm able to use more of myself in dance. Dance is everything: mind, spirit, and body working together with incredible music. It creates something people like to watch and are inspired by. There's nothing better, even on the hard days."

DANCE TALK   **STARTING MODERN**

It might seem crazy to start modern dance in college, as David did, and hope to make it as a modern dancer, but it's not unusual. Experts feel it's best not to start modern when you're very young. "With modern, you need to be older and more mature because the movement is very sophisticated," says Franco De Vita of American Ballet Theatre's school, which offers modern to its teen ballet students. Shelly Power adds, "At Houston Ballet, our main goal is for students to learn ballet first. We begin them in modern at age eleven and twelve, when they are able to incorporate abstract thinking as well as such technical concepts as Martha Graham's idea of 'contraction and release.' A modern teacher might ask you to fall and roll on the floor, showing the force of gravity pulling you to the ground. You have to have developed a certain level of abstract thinking to do that."

The Ailey School starts youngsters at about age ten with a modern technique developed by Lester Horton. It's a very physical technique that the school has found is accessible and enjoyable for kids that age, but the school waits until students have a clear understanding of Horton technique before introducing the modern techniques of José Limón and Martha Graham.

Julie Tice, age nine, warming up at home for her first recital at her ballet school in Springfield, Illinois.

Julie Tice

MODERN DANCER
PAUL TAYLOR DANCE COMPANY

Grew up in: Petersburg, Illinois
Age she started dance class: 5
Dance schools: Local school in Petersburg; Dance Arts Studio, Springfield, Illinois; University of Michigan (earned a Bachelor of Fine Arts degree); the Taylor School
Studied: Ballet, modern, tap, jazz
Pet she had as a kid:
Dog named Lightning
Favorite books as a kid:
A Very Young Dancer;
Little House on the Prairie;
Hardy Boys and Nancy Drew mysteries
Other activities as a kid: Biking, hiking, piano and clarinet lessons
Classes she takes now: Ballet, modern
Other activities now: Yoga, Pilates, Gyrotonics, cooking, reading, teaching master classes, going to concerts and dance performances
Music she listens to now to relax: Classical, opera, alternative rock
Professional career: Paul Taylor Dance Company (before that: Taylor 2; freelance dancer)

"What hooked me on dance was the performing," says Julie Tice, who began performing before she even took a dance class. "I saw dance on TV—*Nutcracker*s and *Swan Lake*—and was always dancing around the living room, putting on my own shows. So when I was five, my parents put me in dance class at a local studio. I did a mix of tap, jazz, tumbling, and ballet. I loved it. We had recitals. I was very shy, but when I was dancing, I wasn't shy at all. I felt like my true self came out." If it wasn't recital time, Julie would still perform. "I'd put up sheets in the basement to make a curtain and stage, and do shows with a friend."

Julie grew up in an Illinois farm town and also liked to ride her bike, hike through fields, and jump into hay piles in barns with her friends. But a special performance changed all that when she was eight—not one she was in, but one she saw. Julie and her mom drove about an hour to Springfield, the state capital, to see its ballet company do *Cinderella*. "I sat on the edge of my seat," Julie remembers. "I had never seen ballet live." She wanted to be part of the magic she saw onstage.

The next day, her mom called the studio in Springfield that was connected with the ballet company to find out about classes. Then she had a family meeting. It would be a big commitment

AUDITION ADVICE

MOVING UP: "I was a slow picker-upper," recalls Julie, describing her combination-learning abilities. "I needed to pick up combinations more quickly to audition as a free-lancer. In class, I used to stay in the back row. I was shy. But in auditions, I found if I placed myself in the front row, I *had* to remember the combinations because I couldn't follow any-one else. Moving up front forced me to focus and concentrate."

Julie dancing with Michael Trusnovec in Paul Taylor's Banquet of Vultures, *a hard-hitting piece about war. Julie's character, who represents life and hope, is ultimately destroyed by the forces of evil.*

INSIDE SCOOP
BEING IN A MODERN DANCE COMPANY

GOOD POINTS: "We work a lot. You don't have to have another job, so you can really focus on dance. That's not always the case in some modern dance companies," says Julie. "It's extremely satisfying because of the variety of work we do." Many Taylor pieces are joyous romps; others are on serious topics like war. "We also travel and perform all over the world."

BAD POINTS: "The downside is the touring. You're away from home a lot. There are also injuries because you perform so much. We all understudy parts within the company. It takes a lot of maintenance to keep in shape. It's not just going to work and coming home. I go to a physical therapist when I need to, and I cross-train. You get splits on the soles of your feet because we dance barefoot. We have special tape we put on our feet. My time is limited in how long I can dance so I'll dance through anything."

for everyone if her parents drove Julie to Springfield four or five nights a week for class. Not only would Julie not have much time for biking or hiking, there wouldn't be time for family dinners on weeknights. One brother felt Julie should "go for it." Her other brother wasn't so sure. "Eventually he came around," says Julie. She was thrilled to go to a real ballet studio, even though she found "it wasn't all fun and games."

"DIFFICULT TO GET USED TO"

"The Springfield studio was more formal than what I did before," says Julie. "It had lots of levels of classes. You were placed each year in a class and were expected to learn certain steps at each level. It was a bit difficult to get used to. The teacher was strict, but she was also wonderful. She knew what she had to do to make her students good dancers. You were there to improve. I fit in pretty quickly. I liked the repetition in class. I'm very patient. I think that helps. Also, I could see myself improving."

After a year of this, Julie was performing in Springfield Ballet's *Nutcracker.* By age thirteen, she was in the company's corps de ballet for other shows. "The teacher let you be in the company only if you had good grades. I would stay up late to do homework and then get up early in the morning to finish." But there wasn't time for much besides dance and homework. She quit playing clarinet in her junior high band because going to dance meant she missed too many band concerts. "Dance is so time-consuming. Sometimes I felt bad about this. I remember my mom sitting me down and saying, 'If this isn't what you want to do, don't feel like you have to continue.' But I couldn't imagine not doing dance. I loved my dance friends. My friends from regular school were very supportive. They always came to see my shows. I felt like I was introducing them to dance."

"DANCE BAREFOOT"

"My teacher never made me feel there was a problem being small," says Julie, who has always been short. "She would find a spot for me. I was one of the fairies in *Sleeping Beauty*, but I was never Sleeping Beauty. Sometimes I was disappointed not having the main part, but I realized I wasn't going to be a ballet dancer. I figured that out when I was thirteen. I was thinking seriously about dance as a career and realized I had to consider my physique. I don't have feet like a ballerina. I don't have wonderful extension like a ballerina. But I knew I could move."

She also knew there was more to dancing than ballet.

"During summers, Springfield Ballet had modern dance choreographers give workshops. They were great. It was fun to dance barefoot." At age fifteen, she read in *Dance* magazine about a summer workshop in modern dance at the Jacob's Pillow dance festival in Massachusetts. She applied, got in, and learned Paul Taylor choreography there from a former Taylor dancer. "I fell in love with that kind of dance. It was amazing. A program like that really helps shape how you see your future."

What Julie saw in her future was the possibility of a modern dance career. She also learned from people at Jacob's Pillow that one way to reach that goal was to major in dance at a university with an excellent modern dance program, such as the university she decided to attend, the University of Michigan. "At Michigan, I

TYPICAL DAY

"On a typical day with an evening performance, we often don't have to be at the theater until early afternoon," explains Julie. "I do my regular morning exercises at home for about forty-five minutes. These include physical therapy exercises I've learned through the years and some yoga. I eat a big brunch. When I arrive at the theater, I do a warm-up and then we run through the show. This usually takes a couple of hours. Then I eat a snack, such as a protein bar and a banana, put on my makeup, do my hair, and warm up again. After the show (or after a rehearsal), I always stretch and release all the muscles that I've used. I eat dinner after the show. When I get home, I stretch, ice sore muscles, and do restorative exercises to balance and realign my body before I go to bed."

took modern every day. I also took ballet every day. It was required. Ballet is central to modern dance. You need solid ballet technique to do all those crazy modern moves. The academic courses were great, too. I took English, art, music, and acting."

"IT FELT SO RIGHT"

Like many college dance programs, Michigan brings in people from major dance companies to direct student performances. In Julie's senior year, a dancer from the Paul Taylor company staged one of its most famous pieces, *Esplanade,* a rollicking wonder set to music by Johann Sebastian Bach, in which dancers race barefoot across the stage: running, skipping, tumbling, rolling, and sometimes practically flying. Julie was in *Esplanade.* "It felt so right. I felt so alive."

Seven months after graduating from college, she headed to New York and started taking class at the Paul Taylor studio. The class there mixed basic modern moves with steps from Paul Taylor dances. "Paul was a swimmer before he started dancing. His movement has that same feeling of resistance as you have in water," explains Julie. "The arms are as powerful as the legs."

PERFORMANCE POINTER

FITTING IN: Joining a company means learning its repertory, the dances it performs regularly. "It was a lot to learn," says Julie, of joining the Taylor company. "You watch videotapes, take notes, and look at notes from dancers who have done the parts. There's a lot of care given to each part. People treasure the parts they have and want to give you information if they're passing a part down to you. It was hard to unwind at night, my head was so full of the movement I learned during the day. I went to sleep dreaming about it."

Paul Taylor didn't teach the class, but he sometimes watched and picked students to put "on scholarship." That meant they could take class for free if they worked in the studio office. Julie got on scholarship, but still had to pay for ballet and jazz classes she took elsewhere. So she did part-time office jobs with a temp agency to earn money while also going to dance auditions that she found out about from newspapers or other dancers. "I auditioned for anything and everything. I was terrible at auditions. I got very nervous." After two years of auditoning, she hadn't won any big dancing jobs.

Then she heard that the Taylor junior company— Taylor 2—was having an audition. Paul Taylor would be there, watching as dancers from his company taught people combinations from his pieces. She decided to try. "I was very nervous when I got to the studio for this audition. Then all of a sudden, I got into a different zone mentally and had the best audition ever. I felt comfortable there. I knew some of the faces. I got into Taylor 2! I quit the temp jobs."

SUGAR PLUM SIGHTINGS

"I was nine in my first *Nutcracker,* as the littlest toy soldier at Springfield Ballet," says Julie. "I did that for four years. Then I graduated to other parts and was Clara in high school."

"INDIVIDUALS WITH DISTINCT PERSONALITIES"

After a year in Taylor 2, Julie joined the main company, when she was twenty-five years old. "Luckily I didn't have to audition again. Paul just had me move

Julie seems lighter than air as she sails across the stage in one of Paul Taylor's most exuberantly joyful pieces, Dandelion Wine, *set to music by Pietro Locatelli.*

up to the main company," Julie explains. Being short wasn't a problem with the Taylor company. There was already another short woman in the company, as well as tall and medium-height ones. Size didn't matter. "Paul wants individuals with distinct personalities." Julie's upbeat personality suited her well for a wide range of roles, from those that call for feisty, explosive energy to those that are more playful, as well as ones that call for the gentle, lyrical qualities she learned from all her years of ballet.

"I take ballet every day when we're in rehearsal. Company class isn't ballet. It's Taylor. I take ballet somewhere else. You don't have to take company class every day. I did when I first joined the company, to get the style in my body. As I've grown older, I find it's important to start my day with ballet. I need that outside eye of a teacher to tell me what I'm doing correctly or not. I'm always working on my line and technique. I also cross-train to maintain a healthy body and prevent injuries, doing yoga, Pilates, and Gyrotonics." Julie still loves to perform. "When I perform, I'm totally transformed. I feel like I'm giving something. I love sharing with the audience. That's another reason I love to dance."

DANCE TALK   COLLEGE QUESTIONS

To go to college or not—and if so, when? Julie followed a path taken by many modern dancers, who generally go to college before joining a company. As Julie explains, "Directors of modern dance companies tend to want college-educated people who have experienced a bit of life." Lauren Grant adds, "You can usually be a modern dancer for longer than you can be a ballet dancer." There's not as much pressure to start as a teen.

Gillian Murphy took a route typical of dancers at top ballet companies like American Ballet Theatre or New York City Ballet. Dancers in these high-powered ballet companies are usually hired right out of high school; they may do college later, either by waiting until their performance careers end or by taking courses in their spare time, as Gillian does. Many dancers in top companies also trained at the companies' schools. For example, nearly all New York City Ballet dancers trained at SAB. However, some ballet dancers do go to college first; you'll meet one of them later in this book. To see which companies tend to hire college grads, check out the dancer profiles on dance company Web sites.

"When you go to college for dance, you're realistic enough to know you're not going to be a performer all your life. You're planning for your future by taking academic courses so if you're injured and your career is over before you thought it would be, there are other things you can do. We encourage our students to be realistic about the assets they have, to work on the ones they don't have, and to look for companies suited for them," says Doricha Sales, who teaches in Indiana University's ballet department. Rima Faber of the National Dance Education Organization notes, "Not every dancer wants to be in a top ballet company, with the pressures that entails."

Not every student even wants a performance career. College graduates can move into other aspects of dance—teaching and administration—or they can dance in college and do something else after. "We encourage our students to go to college, especially if they don't have a clear sense of what they want to do," notes Melanie Person, co-director of The Ailey School's Junior Division. "It gives them four years to figure things out, meet choreographers, and get a lot of exposure they might not get on their own."

Glenn took dance at his regular schools from fifth grade through high school. Here he is at a school performance, with blue glitter on his shoes, dancing to the song "Blue Suede Shoes."

Glenn Allen Sims

MODERN DANCER
ALVIN AILEY AMERICAN DANCE THEATER

Grew up in: Long Branch, New Jersey

Age he started dance class: 9

Dance schools: Public schools in Long Branch; Academy of Dance Arts; The Juilliard School (working toward a Bachelor of Fine Arts degree)

Studied: Ballet, modern, tap, jazz

Pet he had as a kid: Dog named Flick

Favorite book as a kid: *Charlie and the Chocolate Factory*

Other activities as a kid: Acting, after-school job, drum and clarinet lessons (briefly)

Classes he takes now: Ballet, modern

Pets he has now: Cats named Ginger and Eve

Other activities now: Pilates, Floor-Barre, working out at a gym, swimming, teaching master classes, baking cakes and pies for a baking business he started

Music he listens to now to relax: Jazz, alternative rock, R & B, hip-hop

Professional career: Alvin Ailey American Dance Theater

Glenn Sims wasn't planning to take dance classes, until a new dance teacher showed up at his New Jersey elementary school. "She was really cute," says Glenn, who was a fourth-grader then. He and some buddies developed a huge crush on her. They gave her Valentine's gifts, although they weren't even in her class. They were in other classes in the school's arts program. Glenn was in a singing class and couldn't switch to dance that year, but he was determined to do so the next year.

"You had to audition for her class. In the audition, she had combinations for you to learn so she could see whether you had potential." Seeing a combination and then dancing it was something Glenn had actually been doing on his own since he was six years old. "I spent a lot of time watching music videos on MTV. I would learn the choreography and do little shows at home with my brother and cousins." That helped him at the audition. He made it into his school's dance class in fifth grade.

His schoolboy crush soon cooled, but not his interest in dance. He did mainly jazz and tap in the class, which met every day during school. Students gave performances both in school and at competitions. Glenn also danced in school productions of the musicals *Oliver* and *Annie*. He loved performing. "I always liked being onstage. I've been a ham since I was very young. But I wasn't very verbal as a child. Dancing was a way for me to express myself and be onstage, without having to speak and remember lines."

Glenn dancing in Alvin Ailey's Revelations *with his wife, Linda Celeste Sims, who is also an Ailey dancer.*

His dance teacher soon realized how talented Glenn was and gave him some good advice: To make the most of his abilities, he needed to take more classes after school at nearby studios where he could start tackling a very un-MTV style of dancing—ballet.

"I HAD TO CONQUER IT"

Glenn took his teacher's advice and by age eleven was going to classes every afternoon at the Academy of Dance Arts in nearby Red Bank, studying jazz and tap as well as ballet. He kept taking dance there through high school while continuing to take dance at his middle school and high school.

"I was so into pop music and jazz that at first it was hard to focus on ballet," Glenn recalls. "I was willing to try because my teacher saw something in me and felt ballet would propel me further in the dance world. Because ballet was so intimidating, I knew I had to conquer it. I'm the kind of person that likes to try new things. Ballet was hard because of the strict discipline. But with that discipline, you're able to do other things. It's a great basis for all dance."

Ballet at that academy was especially strict because the teachers used a program developed by the Royal Academy of Dance in England. In this program, there are different levels, each with a set of routines that students have to master in order to go on to the next level. "You keep going over the same combinations, which is great because it makes you strong and gives you a clean base for technique." Glenn had another reason for giving ballet a try: He loved to perform

SUGAR PLUM SIGHTINGS

As a kid, Glenn was in many *Nutcracker* productions at his New Jersey studio, dancing such roles as Rat King, Arabian, and Snow King. During Juilliard, he returned as a guest artist to his old studio, dancing Cavalier, a role he has also done for the company run by Amar Ramasar's uncle.

and wanted to be in the academy's *Nutcracker.* He got his
wish, starting out his first year as the Rat King.

"THE DANCER GUY"

A few years later, good advice from a teacher once again
helped shape Glenn's dance journey. During his junior
year in high school, he was taking modern dance at the
academy. The modern teacher introduced him to a
group he had never seen and didn't know much about:
Alvin Ailey American Dance Theater. She used to dance
with the Ailey junior company, Ailey II. Her advice to
Glenn: Audition for the summer program at the school
the Ailey company has.

He took her advice, auditioned, and got into the
summer program on a scholarship. He loved the classes
in ballet, modern, and jazz that he took in New York
City that summer. He also loved seeing the main Ailey
company in action for the first time, performing its
most famous piece, *Revelations*, a dazzling celebration
of African American culture set to soulful spirituals.

He did so well in the classes that the head of The
Ailey School invited him to stay after the summer and
keep taking class there. But Glenn turned her down. "I
told her I was going into my senior year in high school
and really enjoyed my high school," says Glenn. He
was popular at school, performing in plays and musicals. He was even nominated to be the school's homecoming king his senior year. He didn't win, but he was
in the homecoming court. "It was cool to be nominated.

The homecoming court is all football guys, and here I was, the dancer guy. I played sports in gym class but not on teams because I was focused on dance and had other things to do after school." Besides dance classes, he had a part-time job as a salesperson at a mall.

Although Glenn loved to dance, he wasn't thinking of it as a career. Nobody in his family had ever been a dancer. "After high school, I thought I'd apply to Montclair State University in New Jersey and major in marketing," he says. Then along came another piece of good advice.

"CRISP LEGS AND FAST FOOTWORK"

"My male ballet teacher at the academy asked what I was doing after high school," says Glenn. This teacher's advice: Go to Juilliard. The teacher had earned his college degree at Juilliard, a New York school famous for training excellent musicians, actors, and dancers. He thought Glenn was talented enough to go there. So Glenn auditioned, was accepted, and even won a scholarship. "I was excited. This would be a big opportunity for me."

Even so, he flirted with the idea of skipping Juilliard. In May, after finishing high school, he auditioned for the

Glenn's strong ballet training lets him handle easily the varied dance styles he does with The Alvin Ailey American Dance Theater.

company he had fallen in love with the summer before, Ailey. "There was a slim chance that someone could come out of high school and go directly into Ailey," he notes. However, he didn't make it. So he went to Juilliard after all. "My aim at Juilliard was to refine my technique so I could get into Ailey."

Wise advice from his Juilliard teachers helped him work toward his goal. They said that instead of concentrating mainly on modern, which he was really good at, he should push himself in areas where he wasn't so polished. "To me, ballet became that other area where I needed to push myself. The teachers were great, and I liked the challenge. They forced cleanliness in technique. Alvin Ailey said he wanted his dancers to have a 'ballet bottom' and a 'modern top.' By ballet bottom, he meant the crisp legs and fast footwork you can learn only in ballet class. By modern top, he meant the freedom of the torso [upper body]." Glenn worked hard to get his ballet legs in gear.

"FROM THE PEOPLE . . . TO THE PEOPLE"

After three years at Juilliard, Glenn heard that the main Ailey company had some openings and was holding auditions. At age twenty-two, he was a year away from earning a college degree, but he was impatient to become a pro. He figured he could go back later and finish college. So he auditioned. "You had to do a ballet barre and different parts of the Ailey repertory that they taught you to see how you'd fit into the company." He did well and was asked to come for a "callback," another audition a few weeks later. At the callback, he was invited to join the company.

"I was really excited. This was something I had wanted for so long. The company's repertory is amazing. It's cool to go from ballet to jazz to modern, all in one evening." Glenn's strong ballet technique gives him the flexibility to make those changes easily. He keeps buffing up his skills by regularly taking company class, which at Ailey is usually a ballet class.

CLASS-Y TIP

WORK OUT: "I work out at a gym and lift weights every other day," says Glenn. "I also do Pilates and Floor-Barre, which is like a ballet barre, only you do it lying on the floor. I swim, too. I do all this to balance out my body and to be able to walk down the street and feel like I look good." Clifton Brown, who didn't start working out until he joined Ailey, advises, "For kids, just do push-ups. Don't put too much wear and tear on your body when you're very young."

"I live by Alvin Ailey's motto: 'Dance comes from the people and should be delivered back to the people.' It means a lot to me to convey what I'm feeling onstage and have somebody in the audience feel that, too," says Glenn. "It's worth more than gold to have someone come up after a performance and say, 'That really moved me.' One time a woman who couldn't walk said, 'Watching you onstage, I was able to move in my imagination.' When you hear that, it makes you feel good about what you do."

 DANCE TALK   **COMPETITION DEBATE**

About half the dancers in this book took part in competitions. Like Glenn, they feel these were "great performance experiences." He competed with teams from his regular schools because the head of his dance academy didn't like competitions. Neither does SAB's Kay Mazzo: "Competitions take time away from class." Shelly Power of Houston Ballet's academy says, "Competitions can be useful, but they can swing the other way if that's all a student is thinking about. If there's too much focus on competitions, often a student's training is compromised. Time is spent on tricks and perfecting variations that a student may not be mature enough to manage. Artistry is best learned gradually and should keep pace with a student's technical abilities. If a student or teacher finds competitions valuable, I would advise them to do them in moderation." Mikko Nissinen, Boston Ballet's artistic director, believes "The benefit of competitions is in the preparation. But I'm against them because they feed the star mentality. I'm interested in team-oriented work." Glenn notes another problem: "They're expensive." Gillian Murphy adds, "Enjoy the performance experience, but realize that you don't need a competition to validate you."

Elizabeth Parkinson grew up in Florida and liked being outdoors: swimming, playing tennis, riding horses, or just hanging out, as she's doing here.

Elizabeth Parkinson

FROM BALLET TO MODERN TO BROADWAY

Grew up in: St. Petersburg and Tampa, Florida

Age she started dance class: 13 (took a few classes at age 6)

Dance schools: Tampa Ballet Arts

Studied: Ballet and a little modern as a kid; added jazz as an adult

Pets she had as a kid: Dogs named Tina, Butterbean; cat named Solo

Favorite books as a kid: *The Last of the Really Great Whangdoodles; A Little Princess*

Other activities as a kid: Swimming, tennis, riding horses, playing guitar

Class she takes now: Ballet

Other activities now: Reading, Pilates, yoga, teaching dance, running her own school (Fineline Theatre Arts), playing with her son

Music she listens to now to relax: Classical, folk music, '60s and '70s music

Professional career: Joffrey Ballet; Eliot Feld Ballet; Donald Byrd/The Group; Twyla Tharp Dance Company; *Fosse* and *Movin' Out* (on Broadway); *Garden of Earthly Delights* (off Broadway)

"I hated it," says Elizabeth Parkinson, talking about the first dance class she took at age six. "It was ballet and acrobatics. I didn't want to do somersaults or flip backwards. My mother had thought the class would be good exercise for me, but I pitched fits every time I went. I did about six classes, and that was it." Elizabeth refused to set foot in dance class again for a very long time.

She found other ways to exercise: swimming, playing tennis, and riding horses. "I was outdoors a lot," explains Elizabeth, who grew up in Florida with three sisters and a brother. "I also loved music. My parents had a great music collection. I was always listening to music. I started playing guitar in fourth grade. I liked guitar because it was something I could bring into my room and play in there. I liked to be by myself, reading or playing music."

Her love of music helped change her mind about dance when she finally tried it again, thanks to an older sister's boyfriend, who was a ballet dancer. When he visited the family, he said, "Liz, you have a ballerina's legs. You should take ballet." Elizabeth was thirteen, just starting junior high. "I was shy," she says, "and wasn't involved in team sports or anything special. I thought, 'I'll try it.'"

CLASS-Y TIP

TAKE YOUR TIME: "When I was a kid, I wish I had known what a long time I had," says Elizabeth. "You feel this rush that you have to do this or that by a certain age. You hear about people at sixteen who are in New York City Ballet and you think you have to do that, too. But people have their own time lines. It wasn't until my late twenties when everything came together for me. At forty-one, I was dancing on Broadway!"

She took a class at a local ballet studio—no gymnastics this time. "It was the opposite of my first experience. I loved it. It was so soothing to go into the studio and not have to talk to anyone. I could shut everything out, all the worries I had, what homework I had to do. For the hour of class, I could listen to beautiful music, move to it, and get in touch with my physical self. After a few months, I was taking class every day after school. This time it was my decision to go. My parents drove me there and picked me up, but they never came into the studio. It was totally my thing."

"A LATE STARTER"

Soon Elizabeth didn't have time for guitar anymore or for much of anything else besides ballet and regular school. She loved school and did well at it. Her school friends thought her new interest in dance was great. She worked hard in ballet, too, and seemed well suited for it. "My legs, my feet—I had the right proportions. The turnout was there. I had good extension. I loved adagio. I loved to jump."

But some things were frustrating. "Pirouettes were hard. I'm still not the greatest turner. Pointe work was hard. I have long feet, and it took a long time to

JITTERS BUSTER

PERFECTLY HUMAN: "A lot of dancers are perfectionists and that's great; it will help you get ahead. But it can also hold you back," warns Elizabeth. "My perfectionist streak made me so nervous onstage. It took until my early thirties before I could go onstage and really enjoy myself. What helped was realizing that the more prepared I was, the less nervous I would be. So I would practice as much as I could. Then onstage, I would say to myself, 'People don't want to see someone trying to be perfect. They want to see somebody enjoying herself and communicating.' If you make mistakes, the world doesn't come to an end. Humans aren't perfect. If we were, we'd be robots."

develop the strength for pointe work. There were younger girls in class who were so much more advanced than I was. I was behind. That was hard to handle. But I had a wonderful teacher who would tell me, 'You're a late starter. You're not ready for this. There's no time limit. There's nothing that says you have to have this pirouette by the time you're sixteen.' So I would take a deep breath and try to think of myself as a unique individual and not compare myself to other people. I tried to be patient. That's one of the most difficult things to learn."

After a year of classes, Elizabeth made enough progress to dance corps parts in the company connected with her studio, performing in such ballets as *The Nutcracker* and *Swan Lake.* However, she liked class more than performing. "When I started, I was really nervous when I performed. I didn't want to make mistakes. But in class, I felt carefree. I didn't worry because it didn't matter if I made a mistake in class. I loved to waltz around the studio. I felt suspended in time, as if nothing else existed but that beautiful moment. By the time I was fourteen, I knew I wanted to be a dancer."

"COULDN'T IMAGINE DOING ANYTHING ELSE"

At age fourteen, Elizabeth went to a dance festival and took a master class that set the stage for her future career. The class was taught by Robert Joffrey, founder of the Joffrey Ballet. He invited her to study that summer at a program he ran in Texas. She took his workshop that summer and the next few summers, too. "It was unbelievable how much I learned each summer, how much better I got," she says. She did so well that in her senior year of high school, the Joffrey Ballet offered her a spot in its junior company.

She faced a tough decision. She was the top student in her class at school. Everyone expected her to go to the excellent college where she had been accepted. "But if I went to college, I had no idea what to study. There was nothing I was as passionate about as dancing. I couldn't imagine doing anything else." She kept her options open: She joined the Joffrey at age seventeen but also deferred her college acceptance, meaning she could still go the next year. But by the next year, she realized it still wasn't the right time in her life for college. She was totally focused on dance, hard at work in New York City, the Joffrey's home back then, trying to improve as a dancer.

"I was still behind. I was taken into the company because they saw that I had potential, but it wasn't fully formed yet. There wasn't so much emphasis on perfection at the Joffrey as at a place like ABT. Not that the Joffrey wasn't an intense place, but it had more different kinds of dancers." After two years in the junior company, she moved up to the

SUGAR PLUM SIGHTINGS

Elizabeth, age fourteen, was a boy in the party scene in her first *Nutcracker* at her Florida studio. Later she was the Sugar Plum Fairy and Snow Queen. She did *Nutcrackers* with the Joffrey and was in Donald Byrd's *Harlem Nutcracker*, set to Duke Ellington music.

Elizabeth, age fourteen, at the summer ballet workshop she took that was taught by Robert Joffrey.

main Joffrey company, doing corps and principal roles. She loved the dancing, but after several years the struggle to keep polishing her technique wore her down.

"I CAST A BIG NET"

"The ballet world is not always the warm environment you wish it was," says Elizabeth. "We were friendly in the company, but it was so competitive. We were all so young and exhausted. It was hard to deal with. To be successful in classical ballet, you have to be so focused, so technical. For example, I lived in New York City for a long time before I knew about Broadway musicals. That's ridiculous." At age twenty-six, she decided it was time to do some exploring.

She left the Joffrey and spent two years doing a mix of modern and ballet in a company run by choreographer Eliot Feld. Dancing with this company helped her be a stronger, more athletic dancer, and made her ready to say yes when the Joffrey asked her back to be in *Billboards,* a ballet set to rock music. For two years, she toured the world with this piece. Then it was back to New York for more exploring.

She didn't join another company right away. "I had saved up money on tour and thought, 'I'm just going to branch out and see what happens,'" recalls Elizabeth. "I took jazz dance classes, theater dance classes, acting classes, and singing classes. I cast a big net out there to see what I would get. It was fun." Soon she was putting her new jazz skills to use by performing with Donald Byrd's modern dance company, including appearing in his *Harlem Nutcracker.*

One class she took turned her career around. The teacher invited Elizabeth to be part of a group of

As an eighteen-year-old member of the Joffrey Ballet's corps de ballet, Elizabeth sews ribbons on her pointe shoes, a never-ending task for a ballerina.

Elizabeth transformed herself from a trying-to-be-perfect ballerina to a dazzling Broadway star, seen here in Movin' Out.

dancers who were helping him develop a new show he was creating called *Fosse*, which later moved to Broadway, with Elizabeth in the cast. *Fosse* featured dances that had been created over the years by legendary Broadway choreographer Bob Fosse. Elizabeth was thirty-three when she was in this show, an age at which some dancers are winding down their careers. She was just revving hers up, doing snazzy, show-stopping numbers in this Broadway hit. Her award-winning *Fosse* performance led a few years later to a starring role in another Broadway show—*Movin' Out*—in which her dancing was even more sizzling and earned her more awards.

"TRY NOT TO LIMIT MYSELF"

"Broadway dancing is so much fun," says Elizabeth. "The audiences are wonderful. Ballet audiences are more reserved, but *Movin' Out* audiences were yelling and screaming. It's exhilarating. In *Movin' Out* I danced mainly with a partner, Keith Roberts. I trusted him so much. We did a gymnastics-type of partnering. He'd throw me around, and I'd trust that he was going to catch me. I loved the flying around. It was wild." This was quite a change from the little girl who was afraid to do somersaults.

As terrific as *Movin' Out* was, after two years Elizabeth took a year off for something even more wonderful. She and her husband, dancer Scott Wise, were going to have a baby. They had met when they were in *Fosse*; they were in *Movin' Out* together, too. However, eight weeks after giving birth to her son, Elizabeth was getting back in shape with ballet classes, Pilates, and yoga. A few months later, this forty-year-old new mom was once again flying high in *Movin' Out*. "Being a working mom has been challenging, but it has been good, too. When you're a mother, a lot of stuff that used to bother you doesn't matter because you have a new purpose."

Movin' Out ended its Broadway run about a year after Elizabeth's return, but the show was still being done on tour. Elizabeth joined the touring production for a while, bringing along baby James. Then it was time for more exploring.

She keeps landing performing gigs, dancing at such places as the American Dance Festival, while also trying her hand at choreography, teaching in various programs, and even starting a new arts school in Connecticut with her husband that offers after-school classes in dance, acting, and singing. "I try not to limit myself by saying I'm just going to do one kind of thing. I try to keep myself open to whatever is out there. You never know how things will come together."

 DANCE TALK   **BACKSTAGE PEEK**

"I wish people could see what goes on backstage at a Broadway show because there is backstage choreography," says Elizabeth. "The cast of a show like *Movin' Out* was big, but the theater was small. When people exited the stage, some always walked in one direction and others walked the other way, so we didn't run into each other and be late for our next entrance."

Elizabeth wore a lot of costumes. There was a woman, called a dresser, who kept track of them all. "Her job was to make sure I put on the right costume at the right time so I didn't have to worry about that. I also wore three different wigs. My hair was pin-curled under a wig cap. The wigs went on over the wig cap. I had a wig person who took care of my wigs. We worked together backstage like a team: the dresser, the wig person, and me. We were like a machine, doing the same thing every night. I'd put on tights while the dresser handed me my shoes and the wig person did my wig. It was amazing."

Aesha Ash warming up in a studio at the School of American Ballet, wearing a pair of the leg warmers she likes to knit.

Aesha Ash

FROM JAZZ TO BALLET
. . . AND BACK

Grew up in: Rochester, New York
Age she started dance class: 5
Dance schools: Local studios in Rochester;
School of American Ballet
Studied: Tap, jazz, lyrical, ballet
Pets she had as a kid: Dogs named Buffy,
Rambi, Nino, Shadow, and Spanki
Favorite books as a kid:
Baby-sitters Club books
Other activities as a kid: Knitting, sewing
Class she takes now: Ballet
Other activities now:
Learning other languages, knitting
Music she listens to now to relax:
Anything, from jazz to R & B to classical
Professional career: New York City Ballet; Béjart Ballet
Lausanne; Alonzo King's LINES Ballet; Morphoses

"Mom, you've got to put Aesha in dance!" That's what Aesha Ash's two older sisters kept telling their mom. They had taken dance when they were younger, but had lost interest and stopped. That nearly ruined dance for their mother. She didn't want to spend a lot of money on classes for Aesha only to have her quit, too. The sisters kept bugging their mom. "They saw something in Aesha," her mom recalls. "They said, 'Mom, she's more serious than we were. Look at her.' When we had music on, Aesha would dance around the room. When she saw dance on TV, she wanted to do it." So her mom gave in and let five-year-old Aesha take class at a studio near their home in Rochester, New York. Before long she was taking class nearly every day after school.

"I loved it," says Aesha. "I took jazz, tap, and lyrical [a flowing, emotional kind of jazz dancing]. I liked jazz because of the freedom. It was lively and felt very natural. It was fun. We had recitals, and I did a ton of competitions. I won a lot." Then one day a ballet teacher visited the studio. "She told my mom I had talent and should take ballet. The teacher said even if I wanted to do Broadway, ballet could help." So at age ten, Aesha began taking ballet every afternoon at another studio, while still doing jazz and tap at her old studio.

SUGAR PLUM SIGHTINGS

Aesha was a party child in her first *Nutcracker* in Rochester and moved on to other roles, including Clara. She did tons of *Nutcrackers* at New York City Ballet and has been the Sugar Plum Fairy as a guest artist with other companies.

"I hated ballet," Aesha recalls. "The atmosphere in the ballet studio was so not my personality. Everyone was silent. There was soft music. The teacher spoke softly. Nobody looked like they were having fun. It was so different than a jazz studio, with the music pumping and everyone going with high energy. At first, ballet was just something I did to get better at other forms of dancing."

Gradually her attitude changed. "I started seeing the challenge in it. Ballet was hard and intense. It wasn't as easy for me as jazz and tap. I wanted the challenge. I've always pushed myself. So, when I was thirteen, I stopped jazz and tap to pursue ballet. But my jazz background has made me a more well-rounded dancer." It also helped her blaze a new trail for herself many years later.

"I WANTED TO MAKE A DIFFERENCE"

There was another reason Aesha shifted to ballet as a teenager. "I saw that there were very few women of color in ballet," she says. "I didn't see a lot of ballet performances growing up in Rochester, but I saw ballet on TV. You didn't see blacks in the princess roles. That bothered me. I wanted to show that we can be ethereal, soft, romantic, beautiful, and angelic. I wanted to help change the image of black women in dance. I wanted to make a difference."

At her ballet studio, she had a chance to do the romantic dancing she was interested in by appearing in such ballets as *The Nutcracker* and *A Midsummer Night's Dream.* "Performing brought me so much joy. I'm a timid person, but something happens onstage. I can express myself onstage in a way that I can't in life."

Around the time that Aesha became serious about ballet, her mom overheard other parents at ballet school talking about SAB, the School of American Ballet in New York City, saying that it would be hard for Aesha to get into SAB because she was black. Aesha and her mom were determined to prove them wrong. "My mom is like me," explains Aesha. "If you say no to me, I'm going to show you yes." They hadn't known about SAB, but they found that auditions for SAB's summer course were coming up. So thirteen-year-old Aesha traveled down to New York City to audition. She was accepted into the program for that summer.

"I loved spending the summer there, living in the dorm with other SAB students. There were only one or two black students, but that wasn't a problem." After the summer was over, it was back home to Rochester to start high school. "I had friends at high school, but I didn't have time to be in school clubs because of ballet. I don't feel like I missed out. I wasn't interested in those clubs. Dance was what I preferred."

CLASS-Y TIP

EASE UP: "Improve your technique in class but don't lose the joy you had when you started dancing," advises Aesha. "Take the corrections from the teachers but don't use them to beat up on yourself. I spent years beating up on myself, thinking, 'I'm not good enough.' I was harder on myself than anyone was. I've reprogrammed my way of thinking. Think of corrections as a bonus, things to work on, but don't lose the freedom and the joy."

Aesha dancing with New York City Ballet, partnered by Sébastien Marcovici, in Haiku, *choreographed by Albert Evans.*

However, she had two hobbies that she liked doing in her spare time: sewing and knitting. "I've made so many leg warmers!"

The summer after ninth grade, Aesha was back at SAB. She was there again the summer after tenth grade. That summer, SAB officials invited her to stay on for the school year. "I was ecstatic," she says. For her last two years of high school, Aesha trained at SAB while going to a special New York high school that many SAB students attend. She was flying high, until a teacher's comment laid her low.

"FIGHTING TO GET BETTER"

"I've always had a difficult body to work with, as far as turnout and the shape of my body," explains Aesha. "Genetically, I have a more round shape than the classical form. My legs are more round and curvy." She thought she was making good progress until an SAB teacher said that maybe classical ballet was not for her.

"It's hard to hear that from a teacher you admire. For a week I was in a major depression. I thought, 'What has all this hard work been for?' I can get very low, but when I come up, I come up strong. After that week, I came out fighting and spent the rest of my time at SAB fighting to get better. That gave me so much drive. If it wasn't for what that teacher said, I wouldn't have been able to push myself so hard that people began to see something extra in me."

At the end of each school year, New York City Ballet officials watch a special SAB performance to decide which students to bring into the company. Eighteen-year-old Aesha did an amazing job in this show at the end of her senior year, dancing the spunky lead in the "Rubies" section of Balanchine's *Jewels*. She was invited to join the company as an apprentice. "I was more nervous than excited, feeling that now I really had to prove myself."

"OUT OF THAT BOX"

"There were good and bad times at New York City Ballet," says Aesha, who was soon made an official member of the corps de ballet. "I was there for seven and a half years. A lot of it was a struggle. You're constantly pushing yourself to get better roles and improve your technique. For the most part, people in the corps support each other. It's a combination of support and competition. Being in the corps isn't easy. You're constantly learning and throwing ballets together. You need each other."

Aesha did some soloist and principal roles in addition to her corps work. She was also featured in a DVD the company made: *New York City Ballet Workout 2.* All this performing helped her make

CLASS-Y TIP

ALL THAT JAZZ: "I'm grateful I had a jazz and tap background," says Aesha. "It added to my career as a ballet dancer. When we did modern or jazzy things, it was hard for some dancers to pick up the rhythms, but it felt natural to me. It was also good knowing that if ballet didn't work out, jazz was something I could fall back on."

progress with the goal she had set for herself as a young-ster: to change the image of black women in dance. For most of her time with New York City Ballet, she was its only African American woman. "I would get notes from African American kids and other children of color, espe-cially during *Nutcracker*, saying things like, 'It's so nice to see someone up there dark like me.' You get notes like that and you think, 'Wow! This is important.'"

The company had never had a black principal balle-rina, but one of its male principals, Albert Evans, was black. He liked Aesha's strong sense of style. When he choreographed a piece for the company, he cast Aesha as one of its six dancers. His piece, called *Haiku*, was moody and mysterious, using a mix of ballet and modern dance, with striking, angular moves, and unusual, almost acrobatic lifts.

"I enjoyed this kind of movement so much," says Aesha. "There was more room for me to be myself in a piece like this. I thought, 'I have to do more of this.' In classical ballets, I felt I was in a box. The foot had to be this way, the arm had to be that way. I felt I had so much to give artistically but had all these boundaries around me, with the strictness of the classical form. I wanted to get out of that box."

INSIDE SCOOP
BEING IN A SMALL DANCE COMPANY

GOOD POINTS: LINES Ballet is a small company, with fewer than a dozen dancers. "In a small company you have more oppor-tunities to have solos," explains Aesha. "We toured a lot. That was exciting. You get to see the world."

BAD POINTS: "We didn't have understudies. We worked all the time. Touring isn't easy. It's hard to live out of a suitcase. I had an apartment in San Francisco, but I saw it only once every in a while."

"FINDING MYSELF"

After having a talk with New York City Ballet's artistic director, Aesha realized that although he liked her dancing, he wasn't going to make her a soloist or principal. That, combined with her desire "to get out of the classical mindset," led her to leave the company and head to Europe to dance for two years with choreographer Maurice Béjart's company in Switzerland, Béjart Ballet Lausanne. "But I wasn't given the artistic food I was looking for there either."

As she was deciding to leave this Swiss company and maybe quit dance altogether, she met a dancer who told her about a company that might be perfect for her: LINES Ballet, in San Francisco, a company that mixes ballet with jazz, modern, and other kinds of movement, using music from around the world. There was an opening in the company. This dancer gave Aesha the phone number of the company's founder, choreographer Alonzo King. Aesha called him from Europe.

"I told Alonzo King I was disenchanted with the dance world, that I felt there was this fire inside me but that there were always barriers that were blocking me from expressing myself. He said it sounded like LINES was the place for me. He accepted me into the company over the phone!" A few months later, Aesha, age twenty-seven, flew to San Francisco.

"I started finding myself at LINES Ballet," Aesha explains. "Alonzo King classifies his dances as contemporary ballet. He gives you a lot of freedom as an artist.

Aesha dancing with LINES Ballet in The Moroccan Project, *a piece choreographed by Alonzo King and set to Middle Eastern music.*

One of the first things he had me do was take one of his pieces and improvise [make up moves on the spot]. I've been told what to do for so long that it was scary to jump in and do that. I learned so much there. I was rediscovering myself as an artist, getting back to the joy I had with dance as a kid."

After two years, however, she felt it was time to move on again. "I'm still searching. I have this curiosity about what else is out there. I'm getting older. If I want to experience different things in dance and work with different choreographers, I need to do it now before my performing career ends." Soon after leaving LINES, she had an opportunity to dance with a brand-new ballet company, Morphoses, started by young, up-and-coming choreographer Christopher Wheeldon. He danced with New York City Ballet when Aesha was there but had switched to being a choreographer. "I love his pieces," says Aesha. "Let's see where it goes from here."

 DANCE TALK   **CORRECTIONS, CORRECTIONS**

As Aesha found, corrections in class are a never-ending part of a dancer's life and can be tough to take. Elizabeth Parkinson agrees: "It's hard always having someone scrutinizing you, never being quite good enough, constantly being confronted with what's not right. You have to trust that the teachers really are trying to help make you wonderful." Melanie Person, who teaches ballet at The Ailey School, points out, "In dance we're always trying to achieve perfection, but can anyone ever be perfect? There's always something else you can work on, another detail, as the technique builds and grows."

Indiana University's Doricha Sales adds, "You need to be self-critical, but do so in a balanced way. If a teacher is all over you today because you couldn't do something, you can be upset for the moment, but then let it go. Don't take it home with you. Don't say, 'If only I had more turnout, I'd be a better person.' Instead say, 'Okay, I don't have the greatest turnout. Let's see how I can increase the use of the turnout I have.' Enhance what you have."

"*I was always very curious as a kid,*" *recalls Jamal Story.* "*I wore people out with questions. I was also a Lego and Construx person. I'd do the projects on the box and then I'd totally make up my own thing.*"

Jamal Story

FROM MODERN TO BROADWAY, BY WAY OF THE STARS

Grew up in:
Carson, California
Age he started dance class: 14
Dance schools: California State University,
Dominguez Hills; Southern Methodist University
(earned two Bachelor of Fine Arts degrees, in dance and in communication)
Studied: Ballet, jazz, modern
Favorite books as a kid: *Superfudge*; *A Wrinkle in Time*; *Charlie and the Chocolate Factory*; *Bunnicula*; *The Celery Stalks at Midnight*; R. L. Stine mysteries
Other activities as a kid: Gymnastics, piano, Legos, musicals, writing for a local paper
Classes he takes now: Ballet, modern
Other activities now: Reading, writing short stories, singing lessons, working out at a gym
Music he listens to now to relax: Jazz, classical, hip-hop, R & B
Professional career: Madonna's *Drowned World Tour*; Cher's *Living Proof Farewell Tour*; *The Color Purple* (on Broadway); dance companies such as Lula Washington Dance Theatre, Donald Byrd/The Group, and Complexions

Something happened to Jamal Story on his way to becoming a scientist. "I was good in math and science and wanted to be an astronomer, someone who studies the stars," says Jamal. As a little kid, he was always trying to figure out how things worked. "I wore people out with questions." He also loved to read and to create amazing structures out of Legos.

"I wasn't very athletic. Maybe that's why my mother put me in gymnastics when I was eight, to have something physical to do. I loved it. I liked being in the air, the sensation of flipping around." Soon he was training at a gymnastics academy near his home, just outside of Los Angeles. He went to competitions and won medals. "I was told I was Olympics material."

But after four years, Jamal realized, "Gymnastics wasn't for me." He liked mastering the moves but not going for the gold. "Gymnastics is a competitive sport, and I wasn't necessarily interested in winning. I didn't want to put my soul into something that wasn't going to yield anything besides the joy of winning. Also, men's floor exercise has no music, no dancing. I was more interested

---

INSIDE SCOOP
BEING IN A SUPERSTAR TOUR

GOOD POINTS: "The money was great," says Jamal. "There was good camaraderie among the dancers." Cher even went to movies with the dancers. "The touring was great. But what was really wonderful was the energy that came from the audience. Usually in concert dance, you give off more energy than the audience. On tour with artists like Cher, you have 18,000 people in the hall yelling, screaming, and giving you much more energy than you could possibly find in yourself. It feeds you and makes it easier to dance."

BAD POINTS: "Touring gets exhausting, but you have breaks. Artists like Cher don't go out for more than six weeks without a break. You also have days off, with just three or four shows a week." On days off, Jamal wrote short stories.

in what the girls did in their floor routines, performing to music and dancing. That looked like more fun."

At age twelve, he stopped training for gymnastics competitions, although he still worked out at a gym. He switched to activities that let him have fun with music. He started piano lessons. He also joined a musical theater group that met after school and in the summer during junior high, giving kids a chance to learn a little jazz dance, do some singing, and put on shows. He didn't like singing, but he enjoyed dancing and being onstage. He still aimed to be a scientist and went to a math-and-science-oriented high school. But in his first year there, he made a choice that changed everything.

"THE FAST TRACK"

Jamal's high school was on one of the California State University campuses. The high school kids could take dance classes at the university to meet their physical education requirement. "I wanted to do jazz dance, but the dance teacher said I'd be so good at ballet. She insisted I take ballet," Jamal explains. He tried the introductory ballet class and loved it. "Ballet was pretty easy for me. I approached it like a sport, looking for the same things as in gymnastics, going for the biggest, the highest. That

PERFORMANCE POINTER

BE AN ARTIST: "In performance, stop worrying about what you look like, what your leg or foot looks like," says Jamal. "Worry about that when you take class. In performance, have an experience. Be an artist. Trust that those things are there from all the work you've done. Just dance. When you perform, it should be about what you're saying. As a dancer once told me, 'Tell your story.'"

became a roadblock later in my career because dance isn't a sport. It's an art." It took him a long time to learn to use dance to "express something from the inside out."

This introductory class lasted ten weeks, but Jamal wanted to keep going. He signed up to take regular ballet classes at the university after school. "The discipline of ballet attracted me. It was simple, almost mathematical. I liked that." The next year, he formed a dance company with four girls from school. They did a performance at a local mall. After this show, a woman in the audience came up to Jamal. She was from the Lula Washington Dance Theatre, a modern dance company in nearby Los Angeles. The company needed a man for an upcoming performance, just to partner a girl, not to do much dancing. She said it would be easy and asked Jamal if he would do it. So he did this performance and danced so well that the company's founder, African American dancer Lula Washington, invited Jamal to keep dancing with her company, as long as he kept up his grades at school.

For the rest of high school, Jamal went into Los Angeles a few evenings a week to rehearse and perform, while also continuing ballet classes after school. "I took the fast track to professional dancing," he notes. "I was onstage with professional dancers, but I didn't have nearly enough training. It was challenging. I applied my knowledge of my body from gymnastics and imitated what I saw. That's a far cry from artistic dancing, but it worked at the time."

"SENSE OF COMMUNITY"

"Lula Washington's company was my first dance family," notes Jamal. "The sense of community is what I loved about it. The dancing was fun because Lula almost always choreographs things rooted in what's going on, such as the Los Angeles riots. We had a chance to express ourselves on very real matters." When her dancers performed at the International Conference of Blacks in Dance, Jamal went, too. "I saw amazing companies there." He started watching dance videos and going to live performances in Los Angeles by The Alvin Ailey American Dance Theater and other visiting groups. He began to see that there was more to dance than gymnastics-type tricks, that dance was about feelings and communicating.

Jamal explored the expressive side of dance in his senior year of high school when he entered a competition called ACT-SO, sponsored by the civil rights organization, the NAACP. African American students from around the country compete in this contest in various categories. Jamal was a dance contestant that year. He created his own dance solo, wrote words to go with it, and recorded a friend reading the words. He played that tape during his performance, along with a tape of percussion music. His dancing was powerful, but

CLASS-Y TIP

BUSINESS-MINDED: "Be smart about the business side of your career," advises Jamal. "Talk with other dancers. Find how people are managing financially, especially on the small salaries some companies pay. The stuff you need to know to be successful in the business sense is not taught in dance class. You need to learn to make good choices."

more important was the message it delivered. He named his solo *Catharsis*. "It's about black youth trying to find ourselves and not having enough connection with the past to understand what we're doing now or what our potential is in the future." He won the competition.

"FOUND IT"

By his senior year of high school, Jamal no longer aimed to be a scientist, but he hadn't settled on another career. He was good at several things: dance, classical piano, and writing. He was already writing a regular column for teens in a local newspaper. After a while he gave up on the idea of studying music. But he pursued both of his other two interests, earning college degrees in dance and also in communications at Southern Methodist University (SMU) in Dallas, Texas.

At SMU, Jamal took ballet and modern dance as well as academic classes. "It wore me out, but it was wonderful," he recalls. "College teaches you how to learn, gives you organization skills, and prepares you for the real world." He was pretty involved in the real world already. While in college, he became part of the Dallas dance scene, performing as a guest artist with local companies and doing some commercials. He also went back to Los Angeles several times to perform with Lula Washington.

After four years at SMU, Jamal felt he finally "found it"—how to express himself in dance. However, he was tired of the modern pieces SMU did, mainly in the

At Southern Methodist University, Jamal did a lot of modern dance performances, including In a Word, *choreographed by Lynne Taylor-Corbett, in which he danced with fellow student Jill Locke.*

Paul Taylor style. Jamal wanted to do dances like the Ailey company did. He was eager to join a company whose dances reflected more of the African American experience, a company like Donald Byrd's, whose work Jamal had seen at the Blacks in Dance conference he went to with Lula Washington. During his last year at college, Jamal flew to New York to audition for Donald Byrd and was invited to join his company. Jamal was excited, but also a little scared. Donald Byrd was said to be hard to get along with, and his dancers were supposed to be amazing. Jamal called some of the company's former dancers for advice and decided he could handle the challenge.

"NOT JUST A STEP DOER"

"Donald Byrd always had brilliant information to give us, the reasons and thoughts behind the work," says Jamal. "We made sure our actions onstage were human and not just 'dancerly.' We didn't like what we called 'step doers,' people who weren't interested in the art of it, but were just doing the movement. I learned so much. I found I'm not just a step doer."

He may have been learning, but he wasn't earning much, and he had hefty college loans to pay. After two years with Donald Byrd, Jamal auditioned for a better-paying job: Madonna's *Drowned World Tour*. "I heard that Madonna was having an 'open call,' meaning anyone could audition. There was an official *Drowned World Tour* hotline you could call for information."

Hundreds of dancers lined up to audition. Something from Jamal's past helped him stand out from the crowd. Madonna wanted dancers who also had other talents, such as juggling, sword swallowing—or tumbling. Jamal hadn't done gymnastics for years, but he tumbled well in the audition and won the job. The tour lasted only a few months, but "was one of the most amazing experiences of my life." By then he had an agent who helped him get hired to dance for three years in another superstar tour: Cher's *Living Proof Farewell Tour.* On these tours, he did a little jazz and a little hip-hop, along with some gymnastics.

Then a new opportunity popped up, thanks to the wise way he handled things when he left Donald Byrd's company in mid-season to join Madonna. Jamal had found a dancer to take his place, but for an important performance, Jamal skipped a Madonna rehearsal in Los Angeles, flew to Atlanta where the company was performing, and did the show. "Donald thanked me because a lot of dancers wouldn't have done this." Years later, when Donald Byrd began choreographing a Broadway musical, he asked Jamal to help. The musical was based on a prize-winning book by African American author Alice Walker, *The Color Purple.*

At first, Jamal helped with *The Color Purple* rehearsals. Before long, he was in

SUGAR PLUM SIGHTINGS

Jamal wasn't in a *Nutcracker* until college, when he performed with a company run by one of the university's teachers. He did this after college, too, and later was in Donald Byrd's *Harlem Nutcracker.*

the show, dancing and singing in the ensemble of this Broadway hit. He was also the assistant dance captain, the person who keeps the dancers in tip-top shape, show after show, and helps teach new dancers the choreography. The dancing in *The Color Purple* is the soulful, jazzy kind he loves, dancing that tells a powerful story. "I'm learning to sing better, too," notes Jamal, who started singing lessons. "I have no idea how long I'll be here, but I like it."

TYPICAL DAY

Here's a typical day for Jamal while performing and serving as assistant dance captain in *The Color Purple*:

11:30 A.M. to 12:30 P.M. — Ballet class at a studio in New York City

1:00 P.M. — Arrive at the theater to get ready to help the dance captain run a rehearsal for dancers who are understudies for the show's lead dancers

1:30 to 5:00 P.M. — Understudy rehearsal

5:00 to 7:00 P.M. — Dinner break

7:00 P.M. — Return to the theater and get ready for the performance

7:30 P.M. — Give notes to the show's dancers, if anything needs fixing from the previous night

8:00 to 10:45 P.M. — Perform in *The Color Purple*

DANCE TALK   **WARMING UP**

Some dancers get ready for shows by doing their own individual warm-ups, as Jamal did before his Cher performances. "The special talents dancers brought to the show were so different that your warm-up had to be directed to your own needs," he says. Paul Taylor dancers also do individual warm-ups. As Julie Tice explains, "We all have on headphones. Some do a ballet barre. Others do Pilates or yoga. We warm up onstage to get the feel of the floor because we dance barefoot, and different temperatures can make the floor sticky or slippery." Gillian Murphy stretches before starting a thirty-minute warm-up; she changes her warm-up routine from show to show. But Tess Reichlen does the same ballet barre each time.

Ailey dancers usually warm up as a group by taking a company class in the theater about two hours before a show. So do Mark Morris dancers. "After the class, some of us go onstage and work on tricky parts we're worried about," says Lauren Grant.

One thing they all do: Arrive early. "I get to the theater two hours before a show," notes Tess. "I do my makeup and hair, get dressed, and then warm up." Gillian adds, "You have to be very warm before performing, really get your muscles going." But Julie warns, "Be careful not to warm up too much so you don't exhaust your body before you have a chance to perform."

Sarah Wroth was a busy kid, with ballet, Girl Scouts, biking, tennis, math club, painting, playing with friends, and caring for her kitty, "trying to squeeze as much as I could into a twenty-four hour day. "

$\mathcal{S}$arah $\mathcal{W}$roth

BALLET DANCER
BOSTON BALLET

Grew up in: Poolesville, Maryland
Age she started dance class: 7
Dance schools: Frederick (Maryland) School of
Classical Ballet; Indiana University
(earned a Bachelor of Science degree)
Studied: Ballet, jazz
Pets she had as a kid:
Cats named Mary Kitty, Lizzie, and Darcy
Favorite books as a kid: R. L. Stine books;
Nancy Drew mysteries
Other activities as a kid: Painting, Girl Scouts, biking,
golf, tennis, swimming, school clubs, school plays,
editor-in-chief of high school newspaper
Class she takes now: Ballet
Other activities now: Writing in her journal, writing poetry,
painting, swimming, Pilates, yoga, teaching dance
Music she listens to now to relax:
Soft rock love songs, old rock-and-roll songs
Professional career: Boston Ballet

"There's a videotape of me when I'm seven or eight singing to a recording called *Tina the Ballerina*, singing about how I want to be a ballerina. That's funny, because at that age I never wanted to be a ballerina when I grew up. I wanted to be a doctor or a teacher," explains Sarah Wroth. She started ballet at age seven since her mom wanted Sarah to have an after-school activity that would give her some exercise. "I liked it and thought it was beautiful." But after two years of taking class one or two days a week, she quit. She switched to gymnastics for about a year. But she soon discovered that she hated being upside down. "I didn't like flipping either and realized gymnastics wasn't for me. I missed ballet." So in fourth grade, back to ballet she went, taking class three days a week at her old studio in nearby Frederick, Maryland.

This time, ballet grabbed her more, partly because she was in the studio's *Nutcracker*, but also because of friends she made in class. "They were more into ballet than I was. We inspired each other to try harder. When you realize there are people who can do something better, you think, 'I want to do better, too.' I get annoyed if I'm not good at something. I like the challenge of seeing how I'm going to do in a given situation and how I can improve. Onstage or in the classroom, I always wanted to understand how to succeed and how everything works." That included understanding how to get better at ballet. Her dance teacher had the answer: Take more classes.

"So in sixth grade, I started taking nine or ten

Sarah has been keeping a journal about her experiences as a dancer.

classes a week. I still didn't want to be a professional. But I saw what the classes did for my dancing. I got better. I enjoyed it more. My favorite part was any kind of waltzy thing where I could pretend I was blowing in the breeze. I was never her star pupil. I was never the one people thought was going to do great things. I've always been the one who's there trying every day until all of a sudden people say, 'Whoa, what about her!'"

"AS MUCH AS I COULD"

Sarah didn't let ballet keep her from doing other things. "My life has always been about trying to squeeze as much as I could into a twenty-four-hour day," she explains. She was a Girl Scout in elementary school and found school activities that fit her dance schedule. For example, in sixth grade she was in a math club that met *before* school. In high school, she was editor-in-chief of the school newspaper by doing all her newspaper work during free periods or at lunch.

In middle school, she was in one activity—a school play—that made her skip some ballet classes when she had play rehearsals. "I hated missing class, but I wanted to do the play." She jammed other fun stuff into her free time: making silly videos with a friend, putting on shows at home with her little sister, as well as biking, golf, and tennis. She also loved to paint, an interest she picked up from her mom, who is an artist. Sarah tried a summer dance program once, but didn't like being away from home. So she created her own summer program by taking extra classes at her regular Maryland studio.

"SPREAD MY WINGS"

"My parents told me I had to go to college," says Sarah, who agreed with them. "I didn't think I had a chance of becoming a ballet dancer and never even thought of going to a ballet company after high school. Ballet was an interesting pursuit that I wanted to keep up with while I was in college."

She applied to two colleges with dance programs and was accepted at both. One was near home and was mainly an academic school with dance on the

---

CLASS-Y TIP

UNWIND: "During college, if I had a horrible day or casting was bad, I channeled the disappointment into something productive: I'd take another dance class at night," says Sarah. "Dance is an excellent outlet for expressing what's going on inside. I didn't take the extra class to work on turnout, but to purify everything that was going on in my life. It was just me and the music and the steps. The funny thing was, I improved in those classes. I was like a sponge, having released all that emotional baggage. I was ready for anything. The act of taking class was releasing."

In addition to her corps de ballet work, Sarah sometimes dances soloist roles and also helps teach kids in Boston Ballet's school.

side. The other was Indiana University, far from home, where dance was more front and center. It has an excellent, highly selective ballet program geared to preparing students for professional careers. "This was the hardest decision of my life. I ended up taking advice from my parents to spread my wings a bit and go to Indiana. I hoped it wasn't a fluke and the Indiana people wouldn't say, 'Oops, sorry. We meant to accept another girl.'" It was no fluke. They saw potential in Sarah.

"At Indiana University, I grew up in every way, from confidence in self to reshaping my body. I grew as a person, through friendships and coping and being on my own. As for ballet, when you go from one or two classes a day to doing six hours a day, you get better. I also did Pilates, which transformed my body. Before, I was very muscular, with a lot of raw energy. With Pilates, I learned how to lengthen my muscles. I took a jazz dance class one year, and the teacher made it her mission to make me funky." Sarah also taught dance in a children's program.

"I loved the academic courses, too. I majored in ballet but did a second major in education, taking lots of psychology courses that gave me so much insight into understanding people. College is good for people like me who aren't sure their talent is refined but want to get better." By working extra hard, Sarah earned her degree in three years. She was ready to spread her wings even more and see if she had improved enough to find a job in the ballet world.

"READY FOR THE COMPANY"

"On weekends during my last year at college, friends and I went to auditions for

---

CLASS-Y TIP

GOOD DAY: "My dad plays golf and says if he plays badly on seventeen of the eighteen holes, but one is good, it's a good day," notes Sarah. "The same with ballet class. If you do one thing in class that goes really well, that's enough to keep you coming back. Look out. I've got potential!"

ballet companies," says Sarah. "A group of us came to Boston for an audition at Boston Ballet." About two hundred dancers auditioned that day. They were divided into two groups of about a hundred each. First, one group went into a dance studio to take a class that Boston Ballet staff members watched. After the barre section of class, many dancers were cut (asked to leave). The rest went into the center to learn combinations. More were cut, until only fifteen remained. The company's artistic director, Mikko Nissinen, interviewed these fifteen individually. Then it was time for the next group of a hundred to have their turn.

"Everyone else from Indiana University was in the first group. I was in the second group," Sarah recalls. While her friends auditioned, Sarah sat in a hallway writing in her journal, something her dad suggested she do when she went to college, to record her experiences with dance during college and beyond. "I might have it published someday," she explains.

All her friends were cut after barre. "They came out and said, 'Don't get your hopes up. Just have a good time because you have no shot.' I went in and did the barre. I wasn't cut. I wasn't cut during center either. I was kept until the end. There were fifteen of us left. I was the last of the fifteen called up to talk with Mikko. He said, 'I think

SUGAR PLUM SIGHTINGS

Sarah was in many *Nutcracker* productions as a kid in Maryland, kept doing *Nutcrackers* at Indiana University and at Boston Ballet, and has also gone back to her old Maryland studio as a guest artist.

you're ready for the company here.' My heart fell into my stomach. It was incredible. They took only one dancer that day: me!"

A few months later, Sarah reported for work as an extremely happy twenty-one-year-old member of Boston Ballet's corps de ballet, one of the only college graduates among this company's dancers.

INSIDE SCOOP
BEING IN THE CORPS DE BALLET

GOOD POINTS: "In the corps, you're surrounded by friends," explains Sarah. "Everyone is really good about encouraging everybody else. If you forget something, there's always someone there to keep you on schedule. There's constant entertainment in the girls' dressing room. We read magazines, and someone is always telling a good story."

BAD POINTS: "If you want an opportunity that's beyond corps work, then you're in competition with all these other women who are your friends and want it just as much as you do. Rarely are there open conflicts. It's more a conflict within yourself."

"BE CONFIDENT"

"I'm trying to soak up as much knowledge as I can at Boston Ballet," says Sarah. "I take company class all the time. It's not required, but it's good to go. If you don't, they notice. Casting is done by the director of a piece looking at class and then we audition. But every day is like an audition. There's always someone seeing how you're working or performing." Sarah has done well, dancing some soloist roles in addition to her corps work. She has also been teaching. "As soon as I got in the company, I e-mailed Mikko about teaching in the Boston Ballet School. I've done substitute teaching and teaching in the summer program. I like it, and it makes me feel like more of an asset to the company."

No surprise: She isn't doing only ballet. She's also writing poetry, keeping up her journal, taking yoga, reading books, swimming laps, and making drawings and paintings. "During rehearsals I used to sketch people sitting around the room. I've done some paintings that were auctioned off to benefit the Boston Ballet Dancers Resource Fund. One had a bouquet of flowers on a dressing room table with a pointe shoe and a pack of gum." As a painter, she is good at visually sizing up a scene. "That helps in corps work, to see easily where I fit relative to everyone else. Any kind of outside interest you develop helps your dancing. Be confident, have fun, and always keep learning—that's what it's all about."

DANCE TALK   FINESSING AUDITIONS

"At our auditions, everyone auditions together," explains Mikko Nissinen, artistic director of Boston Ballet. "It doesn't matter if you have three gold medals or danced with Boston Ballet. You come to class, and I assess you on what you do in that class. I look for strong technique, clear musicality, and the ability to bring lots of qualities to the work in a short time. I also look for an individual who is special. Present yourself. It's not just a regular class. It's a class where you perform. Show that you can not only handle the material, but master it. Just doing the moves is not enough. Accent the musicality, give a little artistic interpretation. Do everything that's asked, and then finesse it a little bit more." Franco De Vita, principal of American Ballet Theatre's school, offers a tip for ballet auditions: "Go beautifully dressed, in a nice leotard, and for the girls, with hair beautifully done up and a little makeup, so they can see that you are professional and will look good onstage."

This photo was taken in honor of a tap solo Nick Florez did at age twelve. "I can't believe I thought it would be cool to show all my medals," he says. "I'm wearing someone else's sneakers because I forgot to bring my tap shoes for the photo."

Nick Florez

L.A. DANCER

Grew up in: Kaufman, Texas
Age he started dance class: 6
Dance schools: Local studios in Kaufman and Dallas, Texas; Joe Tremaine Dance Studio
Studied: Ballet, tap, jazz, modern
Pets he had as a kid: Cat named Kitty
Favorite books as a kid: Judy Blume books
Other activities as a kid: Drawing; writing, directing, and acting in school plays
Pets now: Dogs named Phoebe and Mona
Class he takes now: Yoga
Other activities now: Teaching with Co.Dance Conventions, freelance choreographer in Los Angeles (L.A.) and elsewhere, taking acting lessons
Music he listens to now to relax: Easy listening/ambiance music; Ella Fitzgerald jazz vocals
Professional career: Has danced on tour with such stars as Britney Spears and Janet Jackson, as well as in music videos for Selena, Britney Spears, Janet Jackson, Will Smith, Jordan Knight, Smashmouth, and others; has been in commercials and performed on TV shows, including *The Oprah Winfrey Show*, BET Awards, MTV Awards, and Grammy Awards.

Nick Florez started dance class at age six, thanks to a bold (and risky) move by his older sister Sandra, who was fourteen then. "Without a driver's license, she put me in the car and drove me to the local dance studio and signed me up for class," says Nick. They lived way out in the country, on a chicken farm in central Texas. It was impossible for two kids to walk to the local dance studio. Even so, don't try this at home, kids!

Nick's sister knew dance was his thing. As Nick explains, "Anytime there was music on the radio, it engulfed my body, and I couldn't stop moving. I don't think my parents thought there was anything special about it." But his sister did. So did the teacher at the dance studio. The teacher was astonished at how well Nick could dance already. She told his parents he had amazing potential. That got their attention. "They became the most supportive parents," says Nick. "They understood how much I loved to dance. Because I loved it, they loved it." They also started driving Nick to class.

He took tap and ballet twice a week. "We had recitals and performed at the State Fair of Texas in Dallas. Onstage, I

TYPICAL DAY

Nick Florez spent a week rehearsing eight hours a day (noon to eight P.M.) when he was part of an ensemble that danced on TV on *The Oprah Winfrey Show* with Janet Jackson, who was promoting her album *20 Y.O.* For the first three days of rehearsal, the ensemble practiced by dancing to taped music. "The next couple of days we rehearsed with Janet's live band," explains Nick. "A lot of times, a live band will change the music somewhat, add different accents. We had to re-choreograph some sections. One day, we came two hours early, around ten in the morning for costume fittings. Janet had to check everybody's clothes and approve them. After that, we warmed up, with everybody doing their own warm-up. Then we rehearsed until eight or nine at night."

turned into a different person. It was like Clark Kent going into the phone booth, changing his costume, and coming out a force to be reckoned with. I felt empowered by performing. I saw John Travolta dance in the movie *Staying Alive* when I was in first or second grade. It made a big impact. If people asked what I wanted to be when I grew up, I'd say professional dancer."

His school friends didn't realize that was his goal until a talent show during second grade. Nick danced in the show to a Michael Jackson song. "I didn't have a routine made up. I just danced, improvising. After I finished, the kids started screaming and applauding. From then on, I was known as Nick the Dancer."

"OH, SO THAT'S WHY I'M DOING THIS!"

However, during third grade, the local dance studio closed. "I was devastated," says Nick. He didn't take class for about a year. "I danced on my own at home. If I wasn't dancing, I felt like something was missing." He found other outlets for his creativity, doing drawings in art class, as well as writing, directing, and acting in plays in school. But he missed dance class. So his parents found a new studio that wasn't too far away. By the time he was in fifth grade, he was taking dance class there.

CLASS-Y TIP

WHAT YOU SEE: "Learning to dance comes a lot from what you see," says Nick. "It's important to be around people who are really good because you learn so much faster and your dancing style grows. When I was about twelve, I needed to be at a bigger studio where there were better dancers so I would realize I could be better, too."

Nick showing off one of the cool moves that has helped him win so many dance jobs.

"At this second studio, I began to study jazz. I still took ballet and tap, but I loved jazz the most. The movement is so free and liberating. I liked to dance fast. I loved dancing to popular music." This studio took its students about twice a year to competitions in Dallas. "Professional dancers and choreographers from New York and Los Angeles would teach. That made the professional dance world more real for me. I'm glad we did them only twice a year. To do more would take time away from what I wanted to learn from class. Competitions are great, but your training is more important."

However, in seventh grade, he began skipping some of his dance classes—the ballet ones. "I thought ballet was boring, a waste of time," he says. His teacher knew he still needed ballet but realized her studio wasn't challenging enough for him. At her suggestion, Nick moved to a bigger studio in Dallas, a forty-five-minute drive away. Starting in eighth grade, he took class there several afternoons a week. His mom, dad, and his two older sisters (who had their licenses by then) took turns driving him.

"In Dallas, I was around kids who had been doing a lot of ballet and jazz. They were amazing. Some were better than I was. That really pushed me. I took tap,

AUDITION ADVICE

YOUR OWN THING: "When you don't get an audition, they don't tell you why. You wonder, 'Did I not dance well? Does that mean I shouldn't be a dancer?' In L.A., it rarely has to do with your talent. It just means you're different from what they wanted. You have to be comfortable with what you bring to the table and know there are circumstances that go into the decision that are out of your control. Then you don't feel so defeated. Learning that can make the difference between people who stay and make it a career and people who realize it's not for them."

jazz, modern, and kept on with ballet, too. When I was fifteen, something finally clicked with me and I figured out how ballet helped my other dancing. I thought, 'Oh, so that's why I'm doing this!' I'm so happy my training started with ballet. It's the root of dance and carries through to everything else you do."

Dallas was important in another way: It gave Nick his first taste of being a choreographer, something he would turn to again many years later. His sister Sandra heard that Chuck E. Cheese's restaurants in Dallas wanted some kids to dance in little videos that would be shown in the restaurants. Nick, age thirteen, tried out and got the job. "We filmed about eight videos. By the last ones, I was helping choreograph them. I'd make up some parts on my own and show them to the producers. They loved it." So did Nick.

"I DO NOT WANT TO COME HOME"

"Living in the country, we didn't have cable TV," Nick notes. "But I saw music videos on Friday nights on the video countdown on ABC. If I went to friends' houses and they had MTV, I'd be glued to the screen, watching videos by Paula Abdul, Madonna, and Janet Jackson. I was also inspired by the strong male dancers I saw in movies, such as Gene Kelly in the classic *Singin' in the Rain,* which is often on TV." Several new movies with amazing male dancers came out while Nick was in elementary school and junior high: *White Nights* with Mikhail Baryshnikov and Gregory Hines; *Dirty Dancing* with Patrick Swayze; *Tap* with Gregory Hines and Savion Glover. "Those movies had a huge impact. When I saw them, I'd put on my tap shoes afterwards and start dancing." Another movie also made a big impression: *Truth or Dare*, Madonna's documentary about being on tour with a troupe of dancers. "It helped me decide what kind of dance career I saw for myself. I was more drawn to the commercial dance scene in L.A. and Hollywood rather than going to New York to do Broadway or company work."

In his junior year in high school, Nick had a chance to explore the L.A./Hollywood dance scene when he won a scholarship at a dance convention. The scholarship let him study that summer at choreographer Joe Tremaine's studio in Hollywood, California. "When I got there, I called my parents and said, 'I do not want to come home.' I was seventeen." He had been a good student in high school and needed only one more course to graduate. He could take it by mail from a university. So he stayed in California, won another scholarship to

INSIDE SCOOP
BEING AN L.A. DANCER

GOOD POINTS: "Working in Los Angeles as a dancer gives you the opportunity to learn of other areas where you can use your talents," says Nick. On the set of a film, video, or commercial, dancers see people in many other careers, from actors and camera people to production assistants. "I know dancers who have gone on to become actors, singers, or even costume designers."

BAD POINTS: "It's risky. You never know when the next job is coming. Maybe you'll have a week between jobs or a few months. Use the time off to your advantage. Take acting classes or workshops on making commercials." Or branch out, as Nick has done, into other areas of dance, such as teaching and choreography.

keep training at the Tremaine studio, and earned his high school diploma by mail.

Nick was the youngest person at the studio, studying in a special one-year program. At the end of the year, the studio brought in agents to watch the students in class. Nick signed with one of the agents who really liked his dancing. Then the agent began phoning him up and sending him to auditions in the L.A. area. The first auditions were challenging and a little scary. "The professional dance world was totally different from the dance class world I was used to. It took me a year of going to auditions to really figure out how to audition and win a job."

"GOING TO AUDITIONS"

Here's what Nick learned about auditioning—L.A. style—for commercials and music videos:

CLOTHES: "Usually you don't wear dance clothes to commercial auditions because it's for something that's more 'street.' The agent would give me a rundown on how to dress. After all those years of dancing in class in dance attire it was kind of freeing to break out of all the restrictions. In some jobs you dance in combat boots! At auditions now I usually wear jeans, casual street clothes, and sneakers. In ten years of auditioning in L.A., I've worn my jazz shoes maybe three times."

EDGY: "Sometimes they don't want you to look too trained. They want you to look more edgy and raw. I trained for so many years to look as perfect as possible and then you go to auditions where they want you to act like a pedestrian on the street, yet also do the movement as part of a dance section."

IMPROV: "Often they want you to improvise. I had become so used to executing choreography that I forgot that part of me that I had in second grade when I would go onstage and dance whatever I felt. I had to figure out how to do that again."

RELATIONSHIPS: "A lot of it is about relationships choreographers have with certain dancers. It's hard if you're somebody new that nobody knows. I figured I would have to keep auditioning so they would start to know my face." He also began taking class at other studios, so more people would know him.

TYPE: "Your look is almost more important than how you dance. They might want to hire certain types. They'll separate the dancers and say, 'Let's see the tall guys first. Now let's see the smaller guys.' I'm definitely in the small category." At first, he was also in the young category. "I looked like I was about fourteen," he notes. His looks helped him win—and also *lose*—his first job. It was a music video for a fifteen-year-old pop singer. They wanted young dancers. "Bingo! I was so excited," says Nick. "I went to the audition and they told me I had the job." However, the next morning his agent called to say he no longer had the job! The singer was African American and her mom thought there weren't enough black dancers in the video. So Nick and some other dancers lost out. He felt horrible but kept auditioning. Before long, his looks and his growing self-confidence won him another job. It was in a video featuring music by a fellow Mexican American, the singer Selena. The choreographer was Kenny Ortega, who did the movie *Dirty Dancing.* "On one of my first jobs I got to work with this legend who inspired me to want to dance." Nick was on his way.

"THE UNIVERSAL LANGUAGE"

Nick went on to do many other videos and TV commercials. He has also toured with pop stars Britney Spears and Janet Jackson. "Britney and Janet are so into dance themselves that they're like one of the dancers in their shows. You become their family on the road. It's different if you work with singers who don't dance. Then it's very separate. You're behind them and they turn around at the end of a rehearsal and say 'thanks, guys,' and that's pretty much that. But with singers who dance, they know how hard it is. We did so much with Britney on tour. Janet even took us on vacation." When

SUGAR PLUM SIGHTINGS

In eighth grade, Nick was a party kid in a *Nutcracker* production at his Dallas studio.

In addition to performing, Nick has started to move into choreography.

the tours came to Dallas, Nick was given free tickets for his family. "It was amazing for them to see me in a show with 16,000 people in the audience, to see how this resulted from everything they helped me with."

Nick still loves dancing and is thrilled that "dance jobs keep coming," but he has begun to branch out a bit. "I've kind of fulfilled everything I wanted to do in dance. I'm opening myself up to other forms of expression. I'm taking acting classes and have done commercials in which I'm not dancing at all." He has also started to teach dance, leading master classes at dance conventions around the country. And he is trying his hand at choreography, something he first did as a young teen. Recently, he has been working with fellow L.A. dancer and choreographer Brian Friedman to create new dance routines for some performers. He also enjoys choreographing dances for the students he works with at dance conventions. "With advanced students, I do a routine to Mexican music," notes Nick. "The students love it. Even if you don't understand what the singer is saying in Spanish, through your movement people will get your message. Dance is the universal language."

DANCE TALK   **AGENTS**

Having an agent, as Nick does, helps in both the L.A. and Broadway dance worlds. Choreographers and casting directors tell agents what kind of dancers they need. Then the agents pick dancers who seem to fit the bill and send them to audition. If a dancer gets the job, the agent usually earns 10 percent of the dancer's salary. A dancer should *never* pay an agent anything before getting the job. "That's illegal," explains agent Victoria Morris.

Finding an agent can be hard. Nick found his through the studio where he trained. There are lists of agents in dance magazines, and you could send them a photo and résumé listing your phone number, height, weight, awards, where you trained and danced. If they're interested, they'll call. But Victoria recommends using a more personal approach: "Talk to other dancers. Find out who their agents are. Or ask a teacher or choreographer you've worked with to recommend you to agents they know. If the teacher is someone I know, I'll see the dancer." Nancy Lemenager, the Broadway dancer you'll meet in the next chapter, adds, "If you know somebody who has an agent, they can take your picture to the agent, introduce you, and try to get you in."

However, you don't need an agent to go to an "open call," or to audition for ballet and modern dance companies, or even to try out for the chorus in Broadway shows or in the touring companies for musicals. To find out about these auditions, look in entertainment newspapers, talk with other dancers, or contact the companies. Jamal Story notes, "Agents are helpful in negotiating contracts and in being the 'bad guy' on your behalf with a show's producer so you don't have to do that."

Nancy Lemenager was a champion gymnast, maybe even headed for the Olympics, when she found something she liked more than balance beams and trampolines: dancing.

Nancy Lemenager

BROADWAY DANCER

Grew up in: Worcester, Massachusettes

Age she started dance class: 12

Dance school: Charlotte Klein Dance Center

Studied: Ballet, tap, jazz

Pets she had as a kid: Dog named Sean

Favorite books as a kid: *A Very Young Gymnast*; *A Very Young Dancer*; Nancy Drew books

Other activities as a kid: Gymnastics, helped brothers with their paper routes

Classes she takes now: Ballet, jazz

Other activities now: Pilates, yoga, photography, babysitting for friends, working out at a gym, acting in plays, volunteering at homeless shelters and with the Girls' Club

Music she listens to now to relax: Music from the 1960s and '70s

Professional career: On Broadway: *Movin' Out, Never Gonna Dance, Kiss Me, Kate, Dream, How to Succeed in Business Without Really Trying, Guys and Dolls, Meet Me in St. Louis, Music of the Night*; regional theater: *A Chorus Line, Chicago, Company, Sweet Charity, Damn Yankees, George M, Lady Be Good, Dancing in the Dark, On the Town, She Loves Me*; has also danced in commercials and a few music videos

Dancing didn't thrill Nancy Lemenager when she first gave it a try. This was the dancing she did in gymnastics. Nancy began gymnastics lessons at about age five, after having fun at home doing the cartwheels and back bends her mom taught her. "I loved gymnastics," says Nancy. "I was naturally good at it. I trained a lot, was in competitions all the time, and I won a lot." As part of her floor and balance beam routines, she did a little dancing but didn't like it. "I'd rather swing on the bars or jump on the trampoline."

However, by age twelve, it was gymnastics that didn't thrill her. She had started at a gymnastics school near home in Worcester, Massachusetts. When she was nine years old, she spent a summer away from home getting advanced training in Maryland. She was supposed to stay there during the school year to keep training. "Everyone said if you want to go to the Olympics, this is what you have to do," Nancy explains. But she was homesick and came home. She got her advanced training at a big-time gymnastics school in Boston, an hour's drive away, going there Wednesday nights and on weekends. "I liked having this talent, but it made me feel alone sometimes. Kids at school would be jealous. I would pretend it was no big deal. I didn't talk about it." But kids found out about her medals from articles in the local newspaper.

CLASS-Y TIP

TAKE IT IN: "To learn combinations, figure out how you learn best," advises Nancy. "You might have to slow it down. Or you might learn better by watching in the mirror, seeing somebody else do it. I'll struggle with something, and the next day I'll wake up and be surprised that somehow I know it. Do it over and over and trust that your body is taking it in."

When she was eleven, she tried moving away from home again to train. "But I missed my mom and having a normal life. It became too serious, not fun anymore. At age twelve, I said, 'I don't want to do this anymore.' My parents were upset, but they said, 'If it doesn't make you happy, don't do it.' I thought maybe I just needed a break, a year off, and then I'd go back to gymnastics." But she never went back. During her year off, she tried dance classes at a local dance studio. "A whole new world opened up to me that hadn't been explored before."

"USE MY IMAGINATION"

"In dance, I found a world where I could express myself and use my imagination and be all kinds of different things," notes Nancy. "Dance was not only physical and athletic, it was also expressive. I was fortunate that the dance studio I went to always told stories through dance. We never did choreography just for choreography's sake. I thought, 'Wow, you can tell stories!' That was so exciting and so different from gymnastics. In gymnastics, you don't express yourself or show a lot of feeling. You're so focused and keep your game face on."

Nancy took tap, jazz, and ballet at this studio three days a week. "I struggled

AUDITION ADVICE

ROOM FOR EVERYBODY:

"There's room for everybody," notes Nancy. "There are a lot of good technical dancers. I'm not the best technically. But people don't respond to me for that. They respond to me for what I express when I dance, what I feel. There's a place for every kind of dancer, every kind of look, every kind of size. Everybody's different. Figure out what makes you special. You're not going to be right for everything. They'll like you for what makes you different, what makes you unique."

Nancy in her first leading role on Broadway, in the musical Never Gonna Dance.

with ballet and didn't enjoy it as much as the other classes. The school had a dance company, and if you wanted to be in the company, it was a requirement to take two ballet classes a week." Nancy wanted to perform, and so she took ballet. The company did several performances a year and a few competitions. "Our performances were mini musicals. We'd tell stories through ten-minute dance pieces."

Nancy wound up feeling that ballet definitely helped. So did all those years of gymnastics. "Gymnastics taught me about conquering fears. It built up strength in my body." Having survived so many gymnastics competitions, she also knew how to keep jitters under control at dance competitions. "Gymnastics competitions were more aggressive and intense because you could fall and hurt yourself. A dance competition could be nerve-wracking, but it was nothing like being up on a four-inch balance beam."

"TRY IT OUT"

Nancy won awards at dance competitions, but this didn't cause a problem with school friends, as gymnastics had. Maybe it was because everyone was

---

INSIDE SCOOP
BEING IN A BROADWAY CHORUS

GOOD POINTS: "I was always amazed that I got to go to work, do what I loved, and got paid for it," says Nancy. "If you love it, it's fun. In whatever show you're doing, you have an extended family in the cast. You have parties, celebrate everybody's birthday. There's a Broadway community you can get involved with that has a lot of fund-raisers and charity events."

BAD POINTS: "When a show ends, it's over," notes Nancy. No more big family because everybody moves to different shows. "It's so unstable. Sometimes I think the people who work aren't necessarily the most talented. They're the ones with the most stamina, who stick it out, have the patience to wait until something comes along. You have to have a life outside of the theater: friends, hobbies, other things you do that excite you."

older and more mature, or because there weren't so many articles about her in the paper. "My school friends came to some of my performances," she recalls.

However, there were some dance competitions Nancy didn't win, such as the time she was first runner-up for Miss Dance of New England. As disappointing as that was, she felt it was helpful. "Losing is painful, but it's part of the process. You have to learn how to win and how to lose. It's good preparation for a dancer's life. You can go to hundreds of auditions as a professional dancer before you get a job."

Nancy got a taste of the winning-and-losing side of professional dancing during her last two years in high school. The head teacher at her studio knew a commercial agent in New York City who set up auditions for Nancy and some of the other students. The girls took a train into New York a few times to audition for commercials. "I did a couple of commercials. It was fun," says Nancy. The teacher's daughter was in the touring company of *A Chorus Line*, and hearing about her experiences helped Nancy learn a bit about what life as a dancer in a musical was like.

When it was time for college, Nancy applied to a few with dance programs. "They were geared to ballet and modern. I didn't want that. I wanted to do musicals." Instead of college, Nancy moved to New York City after high school. "Not every kid is ready to move to New York at eighteen, but I was. I thought I'll dance for five years and try it out. Then I'll go home and do something else." More than fifteen years later, she was still there, still loving it.

"TRIPLE THREAT"

Nancy arrived in New York and immediately started taking classes in musical-theater-type dancing. She had a commercial agent who sent her on auditions for commercials. She didn't have a theater agent yet, but still went to auditions for Broadway shows, finding out about them from newspapers and other dancers. It was so exciting that even losing out at auditions didn't get her down. "You're young and have so much energy that you just go, 'Okay, where's the next one?'" Nancy recalls. After six months of auditioning, Nancy landed a job dancing in the chorus (ensemble) of a musical, *Meet Me in St. Louis.* "I was nineteen and in a Broadway show. It was really fun."

Next, she was in the ensemble of other Broadway hits, such as *Guys and Dolls* and *How to Succeed in Business Without Really Trying.* She did commercials and made a few music videos. "I don't have the edgy look they like in music videos. So that wasn't a strong market for me." To open up more opportunities in the market that was strong for her—musicals—she began taking singing and acting lessons so she could be a "triple threat." That's a

SUGAR PLUM SIGHTINGS FINAL TALLY:

Nancy wasn't in a real *Nutcracker* as a kid, but she was in a spoof called *Nuts and Crackers.* The other three who weren't in *The Nutcracker* as kids are Lauren Grant, Amar Ramasar, and Jamal Story.

Nancy (fifth from left) in the ensemble of a musical she did on Broadway, How to Succeed in Business Without Really Trying.

performer who can dance, act, and sing. Another wise strategy was to take classes taught by choreographers. "If they like you, they'll have you do projects."

After years of dancing in shows' ensembles, she was ready to try landing a leading role. "When you move out of the ensemble into leading parts, you have to own the role in a different way, really take the stage, not shy away from it," she explains. She eased her way into this new type of performing by first doing little featured parts while still in a show's ensemble. Then, she did leading roles at regional theaters outside of New York City so she could practice away from the pressures of Broadway.

To make ends meet, because leading roles come along less often than chorus jobs, Nancy got certified as a Pilates instructor and did some teaching between jobs.

Finally, at age thirty-three, this spunky dancer was ready. A choreographer she knew was doing a workshop that might become a Broadway show. She called and asked to audition. She got into the workshop, which did turn into a show on Broadway called *Never Gonna Dance*. Nancy was the show's lead dancer.

"A DIFFERENT PERCEPTION"

"Being the lead in a new Broadway show was terrifying," Nancy says of her starring role in *Never Gonna Dance*. "I'm not going to kid you and say it was all fun. There were a lot of great things about it, but it was definitely hard." Especially hard was that the show's Broadway run lasted only three months. But Nancy was terrific in it. "Once you've done a leading part on Broadway, people have a different perception of you." Choreographers and directors started thinking of her as a leading lady.

Right after *Never Gonna Dance* closed, the musical *Movin' Out* needed someone to fill in for its leading lady, Elizabeth Parkinson, who was taking a year off for the birth of her baby. By then Nancy had a theater agent who got Nancy a *Movin' Out* audition. Nancy aced the audition and took over Elizabeth's starring role. Nancy's bold, brassy exuberance was perfect for *Movin' Out*. With her gymnastics background, she was ready for the show's wild leaps and spins. "It was hard on my body, but it was exhilarating."

When Elizabeth returned to *Movin' Out,* Nancy headed off to do lead roles in regional theater productions of shows like *A Chorus Line, Chicago,* and *Sweet Charity,* hoping to star on Broadway again one day. "I don't think I'd do ensemble again. It would confuse people who hire you. They'd think you'd settle for ensemble."

While waiting for leading dance roles to come her way, she is exploring another way to "express myself and use my imagination," which is what she loved so much about performing when she began taking dance classes as a teen. Instead of doing this only through dance, she is also expressing herself through acting and has started being cast in roles in plays that have absolutely no dancing at all.

DANCE TALK   **MOVING ON**

A dancer's performing career doesn't last forever, something Nancy and Nick Florez realize as they start making plans for what might come next. On average, professional dancers stop in their early to mid thirties, according to a recent survey. But some performers dance much longer, such as Lauren Anderson and Elizabeth Parkinson, still dancing up a storm in their forties. Other over-forty dancers who still perform include ballet star Mikhail Baryshnikov and modern dancer Gus Solomons Jr., who is in his sixties and has actually started a dance company for older dancers. However, neither of these two men dances full time now; both have "day jobs." Gus Solomons Jr. teaches dance at NYU and writes for *Dance* magazine; Mikhail Baryshnikov runs an arts center in New York City.

Many dancers stay in dance-related fields after their performing careers wind down, becoming dance teachers, choreographers, or Pilates and yoga instructors. Former ABT ballerina Rachel Moore found a special way to stay in dance after a foot injury ended her career in her early twenties. She went to college, earned a master's degree in arts administration, and returned to ABT in 2005 as its executive director.

Some former dancers move into totally different fields, from makeup artist to business owner. "Many become counselors of varying kinds, going to college to train as social workers, psychologists, physical therapists, or movement therapists," explains Lauren Gordon of Career Transition for Dancers, a group that helps dancers plan for their next step. "It's smart to hire former dancers," notes Victoria Morris, who danced for ten years in Los Angeles before becoming an agent. "Dancers are disciplined, take criticism well, and understand what it is to work hard."

Victoria still takes class. So do many people who studied dance as kids but decided not to pursue careers as professional dancers, people like Reka Simonsen, the editor who helped bring you this book and who still takes class about once a week. As Victoria says, "Everybody should dance. Everybody should know what it's like to move to music and communicate through dance. It's great!"

Gillian Murphy in an American Ballet Theatre production of Ballet Imperial.

Glossary

Styles of Dancing
Descriptions of the dancing styles mentioned in the book

Ballet dancing
A graceful, elegant style of dance that is based on a formal set of movements with French names. Ballet was developed in France more than three hundred years ago, with a new element added about 175 years ago of women dancing "on pointe" (on their toes in special slippers). A key element involves developing "turnout," rotating the legs at the hips so that when standing with heels together the toes of each foot point directly out to the side. In the early twentieth century, ballet dancing was done mainly in romantic story pieces, such as *Swan Lake*, *Sleeping Beauty*, and *Romeo and Juliet*, but in recent years ballet dancing has appeared quite often in performances that have no stories and in which elements of other dance styles are also used, such as modern and jazz dance.

Ballroom dancing
Dances such as the waltz or tango, done in pairs, often in social settings (parties or fancy-dress balls) but also sometimes in ballet performances, and in recent years on TV reality shows.

Breakdancing
An energetic street style of dancing to hip-hop music that involves such daring moves as dancers diving to the floor and spinning around on their shoulders or heads. (SEE Hip-hop dancing.)

Creative movement
Fun movement activities for children too young for formal dance classes.

Disco dancing
Flashy dancing to the driving beat of disco music (by such groups as the Bee Gees) that became popular in the 1970s; featured in the movie *Saturday Night Fever.*

Flamenco
A traditional Spanish dance that includes dramatic foot stamping and is sometimes accompanied by the playing of castanets, small shell-shaped objects that are tied together, held in the hands, and tapped to make a clacking sound.

Hip-hop dancing
A bold, energetic street style of dancing that started in the 1970s as part of the rap music explosion and that encompasses several different kinds of movement, including breakdancing (see above) and popping (fast, robotlike moves). Hip-hop dancing can be seen in music videos, in the backup dancing for performances by pop and rap stars, in some Broadway musicals, and even in modern dance performances, such as in a piece called *Love Stories* by The Alvin Ailey American Dance Theater.

Jazz dancing
A sassy style that is often high-energy but can also be smooth and mellow, with swiveling hips and undulating bodies shimmying, shaking, and strutting to the beat of a range of music, from jazz and blues to show tunes or funky pop hits. A key element is a technique called "isolation," moving one part of the body—such as a shoulder or the pelvis—while holding the rest of the body still, giving a quirky feel to the movement. Jazz dancing can be seen in Broadway musicals such as in those by famous jazz dance choreographers Bob Fosse (*Chicago*) and Jerome Robbins (*West Side Story*) as well as in music videos or in the backup dancing done for such pop stars as Janet Jackson and Madonna.

Lyrical dancing
A kind of jazz dancing that is more mellow and emotional, rather than bold and brassy.

Modern dancing

A type of dance whose development began in the early twentieth century with such pioneering choreographers as Martha Graham, who wanted a less formal kind of dance than ballet. She aimed to create a style of dance that would allow performers to exhibit greater freedom and flexibility of movement, especially in the upper body, and that would also not require them to develop extreme turnout. Modern dancers often perform barefoot—definitely not on pointe—with the goal in performances usually being to express emotions, not to tell romantic stories. Modern dancers often use a key element of Martha Graham's technique known as "contraction and release" (contracting certain muscles, such as those in the upper body so that it curves inward, and then releasing the muscles and springing into action), but may also use a range of other techniques developed by choreographers who shared Martha Graham's interest in a more flexible movement style, such as Lester Horton, José Limón, Katherine Dunham, Alvin Ailey, and Paul Taylor.

Tap dancing

Dancing in special shoes with small metal plates attached to the soles of the shoes at the toe and heel, which allow the dancer to make a clacking sound to tap out rhythms. Tap was popular from the 1920s to the 1950s with performances and movies featuring such tap greats as Bill "Bojangles" Robinson, Fred Astaire, and Gene Kelly. Tap became less popular for a number of years but has been making a comeback recently thanks to such innovative new tap artists as Savion Glover, who has shown that tap can be done to any kind of music, from pop and jazz to classical.

OTHER TERMS

Definitions of other terms or abbreviations used in the book

ABT

American Ballet Theatre.

ACT-SO

Afro-Academic, Cultural, Technological Scientific Olympics, a competition for African American youth sponsored by the NAACP. (SEE NAACP.)

Adagio
"Slowly" in Italian; the part of ballet class when students work on developing fluidity of motion in a variety of ways, including practicing extension, slowly lifting a leg as high as possible and holding it in various positions.

Agent
Someone who helps a dancer (or actor, writer, athlete, or other professional) find a job and is paid part of the salary the client earns from that job.

Anorexia
An eating disorder described by the National Institutes of Health as "characterized by refusal to stay at even the minimum body weight considered normal for the person's age and height. Other symptoms of the disorder include an intense fear of weight gain and distorted body image."

Apprentice
A trainee who learns on the job under the supervision of professionals.

Ballet mistress/master
A person in a ballet company who supervises rehearsals and helps dancers learn the steps in the company's repertory.

Barre
"Bar" in French; a wooden bar dancers hold for balance while doing exercises; also refers to the beginning part of a ballet class, during which students hold on to the wooden bar during warm-up exercises.

Body mass index (BMI)
A way of assessing body fat by using a mathematical formula that takes into account a person's height and weight.

Boogie board
Small rectangular-shaped foam board used to ride waves, in surfing.

Broadway theaters
Theaters where musicals (and plays) are done in a district of New York City near Times Square. (SEE Musicals.)

Character classes
Dance classes that teach regional folk dances such as flamenco. (SEE Flamenco.)

Choreographer
Someone who puts together steps and other movements in order to create a dance piece; these steps and movements are called the piece's "choreography."

Chorus
In musical theater, dancers and/or singers who perform as a group in support of the main characters; also called the ensemble.

Classical ballet
Ballet performances, usually with elaborate costumes, of such romantic stories as *Swan Lake, Sleeping Beauty,* and *Romeo and Juliet,* with dancers using formal ballet technique, including ballerinas dancing "on pointe." (SEE Ballet dancing and Pointe.)

Combination
A series of dance steps.

Commercial dance
Dancing jobs for such things as TV commercials, music videos, movies, special shows put on for conventions, and touring performances by pop stars.

Company class
A dance class that a dance company's members take together.

Concert dance
Performances done by a ballet or modern dance company, as opposed to dance that's part of a Broadway musical or music video.

Contemporary ballet
Dance pieces that mix a variety of styles, such as ballet, modern, and jazz.

Corps de ballet
The large group of dancers in a ballet company who usually perform in a group as a background for the soloists and principal dancers.

Cross-train
To train in different kinds of movement techniques—such as swimming, Pilates, Gyrotonics, or yoga—in addition to dance, so as to develop a wider range of muscle strength than if training is limited to just one type of exercise. (SEE Pilates; Gyrotonics; Yoga.)

Dance captain
The dancer in a Broadway show who conducts brush-up rehearsals during the show's run and who may also audition, hire, and train new dancers when the choreographer and director are not available.

Dehydrated
Not having enough water in your body.

Double tour en l'air
Double turn, while jumping in the air; *tour* in French means "turn" and *en l'air* means "in the air."

Elliptical trainer
A piece of exercise equipment that has a person do walking or running movements.

Ensemble
SEE Chorus.

Extension
In dance, how high a leg can be lifted.

Floor-Barre
An exercise system in which dancers lie on the floor and do the same kinds of exercises usually done standing at the barre in ballet class.

Fouetté
"Whipped" in French; in *Swan Lake* this term refers to a turn in which the moving leg uses a whipping motion to propel the body around.

Freelance dancer
Someone who performs for various dance companies without being a permanent member of them.

GED
The General Educational Development testing program, which assesses basic skills and lets students who pass the test have a certificate regarded as equivalent to a high school diploma; minimum age to take the test varies.

Gig
A job (pronounced with a hard *g* as in "girl").

Gyrotonics
An exercise system in which people make circular movements using a special machine.

Improvise
To make up a dance (or anything else) on the spur of the moment.

Jackson International Competition
The USA International Ballet Competition, which takes place every four years in Jackson, Mississippi.

Line
In dance, arranging all parts of the body to form a pleasing, graceful-looking shape.

Mark
In dance, dancing with only partial energy, not full-out.

Master class
A special one-time class taught by a guest artist.

Musicals
Shows that combine acting, singing, music, and dance to tell a story, such as *A Chorus Line*, *Les Misérables*, *Cats*, and *The Color Purple*, which are performed in New York City in top Broadway theaters as well as in movies, and also in other theaters around the country, including maybe even in your own school's auditorium! (SEE Broadway theaters.)

NAACP
National Association for the Advancement of Colored People, a major civil rights organization.

NCSA
North Carolina School of the Arts.

Nutritionist
Someone trained to help people plan how to eat healthy diets.

Open call
An audition open to anyone, whether the person has an agent or not.

Pas de deux
"Step for two" in French; a dance for two people.

Physical therapy
Treatments by trained professionals with the aim of maintaining or restoring a person's ability to move well, using exercises, massage, and other methods.

Pilates
A system of exercises that tends to strengthen muscles without bulking them up, with some exercises being done on mats, while others are done on special machines.

Pirouette
In ballet, a complete turn of the body while standing on one foot.

Pointe
In ballet, dancing on the toes in hardened ballet slippers called pointe shoes.

Port de bras
"Carrying of the arms" in French; the movements of the arms in ballet.

Principal dancer
The highest-level performer in many ballet companies.

Prix de Lausanne
A ballet competition in Lausanne, Switzerland, for students of all nationalities, age fifteen to seventeen, who have not yet been employed professionally; in French *prix* means "prize."

R & B
Rhythm and blues; a style of pop music.

Repertory
The pieces a dance company performs.

SAB
School of American Ballet.

Soloist
The second-highest level of dancer in many ballet companies; someone who performs solos, dancing alone or with one partner.

Touring
Traveling to other cities or towns to perform.

Triple threat
A performer who can sing, dance, and act.

Turnout
In ballet, rotating the legs at the hips so that when one stands with heels together, the toes on each foot point directly out to the side.

Understudy
A performer who learns a part in order to take over if the performer who regularly does that part can't do it for some reason.

Yoga
An exercise system originally from India that promotes calmness and concentration.

Resources

Dance Companies

Here is contact information for the dance companies that figured most prominently in the professional careers of the dancers in this book.

Alonzo King's LINES Ballet
26 Seventh Street
San Francisco, CA 94103
415-863-3040
www.linesballet.org

Alvin Ailey American Dance
   Theater
The Joan Weill Center for Dance
405 West 55th Street
New York, NY 10019
212-405-9000
www.alvinailey.org

American Ballet Theatre (ABT)
890 Broadway
New York, NY 10003
212-477-3030
www.abt.org

Béjart Ballet Lausanne
Chemin du Presbytère
Case postale 25
CH - 1000 Lausanne 22
SUISSE
http://bejart.ch/fr

Boston Ballet
19 Clarendon Street
Boston, MA 02116-6100
617-695-6950
www.bostonballet.org

Co.Dance Conventions
P.O. Box 752830
Memphis, TN 38175
1-888-I Relevé (or 473-5383)
www.codance.com

Donald Byrd/The Group
This company closed in 2002
when Donald Byrd became
artistic director of:
Spectrum Dance Theater
800 Lake Washington Boulevard
Seattle, WA 98122
206-325-4161
www.spectrumdance.org

Eliot Feld's Ballet Tech
890 Broadway
New York, NY 10003
212-777-7710
www.ballettech.org

Houston Ballet
1921 West Bell Street
Houston, TX 77019
713-523-6300
www.houstonballet.org

The Joffrey Ballet
70 East Lake Street, Suite 1300
Chicago, IL 60601
312-739-0120
www.joffrey.com

Lula Washington Dance Theatre
3773 South Crenshaw Boulevard
Los Angeles, CA 90016
323-292-5852
www.lulawashington.com

Mark Morris Dance Group
3 Lafayette Avenue
Brooklyn, NY 11217-1415
718-624-8400
www.markmorrisdancegroup.org

Morphoses/The Wheeldon Company
800 Fifth Avenue, Suite 18F
New York, NY 10021
212-588-9001
www.morphoses.org

New York City Ballet
New York State Theater
20 Lincoln Center
New York, NY 10023
212-870-5500
www.nycb.org

Paul Taylor Dance Company
552 Broadway
New York, NY 10012
212-431-5562
www.ptdc.org

Urban Ballet Theater
5 West 102nd Street, Suite 5B
New York, NY 10025
212-663-7140
www.urbanballettheater.org

ORGANIZATIONS AND WEB SITES

American Ballet Theatre Ballet Dictionary. An online dictionary of ballet terms, with photos and videos of ABT dancers demonstrating many of the moves.
www.abt.org/education/dictionary/index .html

Career Transition for Dancers. A group that helps dancers plan for post-performance careers.
www.careertransition.org

Dance/USA. This group's Web site has a section called Advice for Young Dancers and also lists hundreds of U.S. dance companies and festivals.
www.danceusa.org

National Dance Education Organization (NDEO). This organization promotes excellence in dance education.
www.ndeo.org

National Eating Disorders Association. This group's Web site provides useful information and help in finding professionals who offer treatment and counseling.
www.nationaleatingdisorders.org

National Institute of Mental Health (NIMH). The Web site of this government agency offers information on eating disorders, including a booklet called *Eating Disorders: Facts About Eating Disorders and the Search for Solutions.*
www.nimh.nih.gov/Publicat/eatingdisorders.cfm

FURTHER READING

Magazines

Dance	www.dancemagazine.com	800-331-1750
Dance Spirit	www.dancespirit.com	800-873-9863
Pointe	www.pointemagazine.com	800-532-9572

Advice and Reference Books

Advice for Dancers: Emotional Counsel and Practical Strategies by Linda H. Hamilton (Jossey-Bass Publishers, 1998). Wise words from a psychologist and former New York City Ballet dancer who writes an advice column in *Dance* magazine.

The Ballet Companion: A Dancer's Guide to the Technique, Traditions, and Joys of Ballet by Eliza Gaynor Minden (Simon and Schuster, 2005). A comprehensive reference book with more than 300 pages filled with information on ballet and other forms of dance, along with advice on keeping healthy and dealing with body-image issues.

Dance by Andrée Grau (Alfred A. Knopf, 1998). Part of the Eyewitness Books series, this volume provides information and photographs on various types of dance.

Footnotes: Dancing the World's Best-Loved Ballets by Frank Augustyn and Shelley Tanaka (Millbrook Press, 2001). Ballet history and lore, along with plot summaries of famous ballets.

Getting Started in Ballet: A Parent's Guide to Dance Education by Anna Paskevska (Oxford University Press, 1997). Useful information on how and when to start training not only in ballet but also in modern and other styles; also covers injury prevention, career advice, and eating disorders.

Put Your Best Foot Forward: A Young Dancer's Guide to Life by Suki Schorer (Workman Publishing, 2005). A School of American Ballet teacher offers helpful advice for young ballerinas.

Superguides Ballet by Darcey Bussell (DK Publishing, 2000). This book by a former Royal Ballet ballerina provides photographs of basic ballet positions.

Books on Dancers

Here are a few dance biographies and autobiographies, not written for kids, but filled with fascinating stories about dance.

Dancing Spirit: An Autobiography by Judith Jamison with Howard Kaplan (Doubleday, 1993).

Holding on to the Air: An Autobiography by Suzanne Farrell with Toni Bentley (Summit Books, 1990).

Private Domain: An Autobiography by Paul Taylor (Alfred A. Knopf, 1987).

Prodigal Son: Dancing for Balanchine in a World of Pain and Magic by
  Edward Villella with Larry Kaplan (Simon and Schuster, 1992).
SAVION! My Life in Tap by Savion Glover and Bruce Weber
  (William Morrow and Company, 2000).

Viewing Guide
*Below are DVDs and videos that feature performances by some of the
dancers in this book.*

To see Aesha Ash perform:
Barbie in the Nutcracker, Mattel Entertainment, distributed by
Artisan. (In the More Fun section, you'll find *Living a Ballet
Dream,* a documentary about the School of American Ballet, fea-
turing Aesha Ash.)

To see Clifton Brown and Glenn Allen Sims perform:
Beyond the Steps: Alvin Ailey American Dance Theater, a Bertelsen
Philm, produced and directed by Phil Bertelsen.

To see Gillian Murphy perform:
American Ballet Theatre in Swan Lake, a production of Thir-
teen/WNET New York in association with WETA, distributed
by Image Entertainment. (For more photos of Gillian in action,
visit www.GillianMurphy.com.)

To see videos in which Jamal Story performs:
Cher: The Farewell Tour, produced by Cher, Roger Davies, Lindsay
Scott, and Serpent Films, distributed by Image Entertainment.

To see videos in which Nick Florez performs:
Britney Spears Greatest Hits: My Prerogative, produced by Ann
Carli, A Fuzzy Bunny Films/Relevant Production. Nick Florez is
one of the ensemble dancers in the following pieces on the video:
*Me Against the Music, Oops! I Did It Again, Born to Make You
Happy,* and *(You Drive Me) Crazy.*

*Here are DVDs and videos with performances by some of the other compa-
nies mentioned in this book, although none features any of the book's sixteen
dancers.*

Ailey Dances Starring The Alvin Ailey American Dance Theater, Kultur International Films, Long Branch, New Jersey. (This older video from 1982, which seems to be out of print but is still in some libraries, is probably the one with Donna Wood in *Cry* that Clifton Brown saw as a kid.)

George Balanchine's The Nutcracker, featuring the New York City Ballet, Warner Home Video.

Paul Taylor Dancemaker, a film by Matthew Diamond, distributed by Docudrama. (This gives a backstage look at a dance company, showing how a piece is choreographed and how dancers cope with the muscle pain and injuries that are part of a dancer's life.)

Yo-Yo Ma: Inspired by Bach, a DVD that includes the film *Falling Down Stairs with Mark Morris and the Mark Morris Dance Group,* by Barbara Willis Sweete, produced by Rhombus Media, distributed by Sony Music. (This gives a backstage look at how a piece is choreographed, in this case a dance called *Falling Down Stairs* that Mark Morris created in collaboration with cellist Yo-Yo Ma.)

Acknowledgments

I'm extremely grateful to the sixteen dancers featured in this book. Even though they are amazingly busy, they took time to be interviewed, sharing childhood memories and tips for young dancers, as well as digging into old scrapbooks to come up with precious childhood photos. Thanks also go to the dancers' family members who helped round up those childhood photos, and to the following parents who shared their memories of what it was like to raise a talented young dancer: Lauren Anderson's parents, Doris Parker and Lawrence Anderson; Aesha Ash's mother, Stella Ash; Nancy Lemenager's mother, Lee Lemenager; David Leventhal's mother, Jean Leventhal; Amar Ramasar's mother, Merida Rodriguez; John Selya's mother, Frances Selya; and Sarah Wroth's parents, Dean and Ted Wroth.

Thanks also go to the following dance professionals and educators who shared their views and provided wise suggestions for young dancers: Martie Barylick, Mamaroneck (New York) High School; Franco De Vita, Principal of American Ballet Theatre's Jacqueline Kennedy Onassis School; Rima Faber, Ph.D., Program Director, National Dance Education Organization; Ana Marie Forsythe, teacher, The Ailey School; Lauren Gordon, National Outreach and New York Career Counselor, Career Transition for Dancers; Doug Long, Coordinator, Academic and College Counseling, Interlochen Arts Academy; Kay Mazzo, Co-Chairman of Faculty, School of American Ballet; Mikko Nissinen, Artistic Director, Boston Ballet; Melanie Person, Junior Division Co-Director, The Ailey School; Shelly Power, Associate Director, Houston Ballet Ben Stevenson Academy; Doricha Sales, Ballet Department, Indiana University School of Music. Special thanks goes to dance agent Victoria Morris at Kazarian/Spencer & Associates, Inc., for her enthusiastic support and advice; and also to Eliza Gaynor Minden and Amanda McKerrow, for reviewing the manuscript and offering such warm words of support.

I'm also grateful to the following staff members of various dance companies who helped to arrange the dancer interviews and provide photos from the dancers' professional careers: Alonzo King's LINES Ballet: Robert Rosenwasser; Alvin Ailey American Dance Theater: Cory Greenberg and Lynette P. Rizzo; American Ballet Theatre: Kelly Ryan and Susie Morgan; Boston Ballet: Jo Cardin, Leah Harrison, Elizabeth Olds, Ann Petrucelli and Sharon Rice; Houston Ballet: Melissa Carroll, Cassie Patterson McClung, and Johanna Tschebull; Mark Morris Dance Group: Nancy Umanoff, Christy Bolingbroke, and Adrienne Bryant; Paul Taylor Dance Company: Wallace Chappell, Jennifer Lerner, and Alan Olshan; New York City Ballet: Joe Guttridge and John-Mario Sevilla. Also helpful in providing photos of the dancers: Erin Baiano, Paul Kolnik Studio; Leonard Cardenas, Jenny Cottle, and Jackie Oliva, Janet Botaish Group; Marci Hall and Myra Woodruff, Southern Methodist University Division of Dance; Tracie Marciniak, Co.Dance; Mitsuko Terasawa, Japan Arts Corporation. Thanks to the dance photographers whose wonderful photos appear in the book: Stephanie Berger, Tom Caravaglia, Jo Cardin, Lance Cheshire, Peter DaSilva, Andrew Eccles, Pam Francis, Ken Friedman, Lois Greenfield, Paul Kolnik, Joan Marcus, Nan Melville, Rosalie O'Connor, Eduardo Patino, Jared Redick, Hidemi Seto, Marty Sohl, Martha Swope, Paul Talley, and Geoff Winningham.

The research for this book started almost ten years ago with an informal survey of seventy-five youngsters who were studying dance, to discover what problems they were having in dance class and in coping with the pressures involved in being serious dance students. The areas of concern these youngsters described on their survey forms provided the jumping-off point for this book. The students polled were taking dance classes at Peabody Institute's Preparatory Division, Baltimore, Maryland; Washington School of Ballet, Washington, D.C.; the School of Dance Connecticut, Hartford, Connecticut; Milwaukee High School of the Arts, Milwaukee, Wisconsin; School for Creative and Performing Arts, Cincinnati, Ohio; Mamaroneck High School, Mamaroneck, New York. I'm grateful to the students who shared their thoughts on these survey forms and also to the following teachers who encouraged the students to do so: Carol Bartlett, Martie Barylick, Rex Bickmore, Christine Busch, Devon Carney, Mel Claridge, Dean Drews, and Patricia Rozow. I would also like to thank the following schools for letting me observe classes: The

Ailey School, American Ballet Theatre's Jacqueline Kennedy Onassis School, the School of American Ballet, and Dance Cavise.

Warm thanks also go to the following people who read the manuscript and offered helpful pointers: Martie Barylick, Cory Greenberg, Victoria Morris, and Melanie Person. I'm also grateful for the encouragement and assistance of: Amy Bordy, School of American Ballet; Lourdes Lopez, Morphoses; Joanne Scheuble, Scheuble Communications; Michael Place, Jenna Harju, and Jacole Kitchen of Kazarian/Spencer & Associates, Inc.; Herbert Migdoll, Joffrey Ballet; and, of course, my editor, Reka Simonsen, a former dancer herself, who has offered many valuable and helpful suggestions. I'm also thankful for the support and encouragement of my sons, Eric and Noah, and most especially of my husband, Carl, who has come to love going to dance performances as much as I do. My love of dance started when I was a little girl, taking a bus with my mother early on Saturday mornings so my older sister and I could take ballet classes taught by Michael Nicholoff, a charming and somewhat mysterious teacher who seemed oh-so-sophisticated and brought the magic of ballet to his rather drab little studio in downtown Baltimore. He was said to have danced with the legendary Russian ballerina Anna Pavlova and made us feel that we, too, were a part of the wider world of ballet. I never became a professional dancer, but thanks to those ballet classes I took as a youngster and all the classes in modern dance that I took during college (with Claire Mallardi at Harvard) and for several years after college at various studios, I have become an enthusiastic and appreciative watcher of dance performances.

Index

(Page references in *italic* refer to illustrations.)

A

Abdul, Paula, 180

ABT. *See* American Ballet Theatre

Academy of Dance Arts (Red Bank, N.J.), 122–23, 124, 127

Acceptance in Surrender, 30

Acrobatics, 24

  see also Gymnastics

Acting, 198

  as part of dance performance, 64

  in plays and musicals as kids, 72, 88, 98–99, 120, 123, 155, 168, 177

  training in, 92, 195–96

ACT-SO competition, 157–58

Adagio, 38

African American experience, dances reflecting, 27, 123, 157–58, 160

Agents, 5, 182, 187, 199

Ailey, Alvin, 27, *121,* 126, 127, 203

  see also Alvin Ailey American Dance Theater

Ailey School, The, 29–31, 32, 105, 117, 123, 151

Ailey II company, 123

Allegro, il Penseroso ed il Moderato, L', 103

Alvin Ailey American Dance Theater, 26–32, *28, 30,* 60, *121,* 123, 125, 126–27, 157, 160, 163, 202, 211

American Ballet Theatre (ABT), 2, 4, 6, *11,* 14, *15,* 18, 19, 20, 45, *49,* 50, 53, 54, 57, 60, 73, 81, 117, 133, 199, *200,* 211

  school of, 12, 33, 105

American Ballet Theatre Ballet Dictionary, 213

American Dance Festival, 139

Anderson, Lauren, *34–35, 35–43, 37, 39, 44,* 45, 199

Anderson, Lawrence, *44*

Apprentices, at New York City Ballet, 65, 75, 78, 80, 147

Arms:

  movement of (port de bras), 27

Art, making paintings and drawings, 168, 173, 177

Arts administration, 117, 199

Ash, Aesha, *140–41,* 141–51, *145, 150,* 215

Assistant dance captain, 162

Astaire, Fred, 203

Auditions, 19, 29–31, 63, 91, 114, 160–61, 170–72, 194, 195

  advice for, 32, 101, 108, 173, 179, 182–84

  agents and, 182, 187

  clothes for, 173, 182

  combination-learning abilities and, 32, 91, 108, 120

  dealing with rejection in, 179, 194

Auditions (*cont.*)
L.A. style—for commercials and
music videos, 182–84
nervousness before, 63, 114
open calls and, 160, 187
temp work and, 102

B
Bach, Johann Sebastian, 113
Balanchine, George, 17, *61,* 64, *68,*
85–86, 147
Ballet Arizona (Phoenix), 29
Ballet companies:
corps de ballet dancers in,
19–20, 42, 53, 65–6, 73, 78,
80, 147, 172
principal dancers in, 14, 20
soloists in, 19, 20, 42, 66, 67
see also American Ballet Theatre;
Ballet Arizona; Béjart Ballet
Lausanne; Boston Ballet;
Columbia City Ballet; Dance
Theater of Harlem; Houston
Ballet; Joffrey Ballet; José
Mateo Ballet Theatre; LINES
Ballet; Morphoses; New York
City Ballet; Pennsylvania
Ballet; Urban Ballet
Theater
Ballet dancing, 201
college education and, 20, 67, 69,
117, 168–171
dancer profiles, 9–20, 35–45,
47–57, 59–69, 71–80, 129–39,
141–51, 165–73
late starters and, 72, 75, 81,
130–31
Russian style of, 85, 86
switching to Broadway musicals
from, 54–56, 137–38

switching to modern dance from,
88–89, 99–100, 111–12
training in, important for all
dancers, 25, 29, 32, 33, 56,
105, 113, 116, 121–23,
125–26, 142–43, 155–56,
179–80, 193
Ballet Imperial, 200
Ballet mistresses, 66, 75
Ballroom dancing, 33, 201
Banquet of Vultures, 109
Barre work, 12, 76, 163
Floor-Barre, 126
Barylick, Martie, 33
Baryshnikov, Mikhail, *2,* 4, 50, 51,
53, 57, 181, 199
Béjart, Maurice, 149
Béjart Ballet Lausanne, 149, 211
Ben Stevenson Academy (Houston
Ballet), 33
Bernstein, Leonard, 79
Billboards, 135
Blacks in Dance conference,
157, 160
"Blue Suede Shoes," *118*
Body memory, 12
Body image, dealing with, 93
in L.A./Hollywood dance scene,
183–84
puberty and, 93
round and curvy shape and, 146
short, muscular build and, 53, 84,
87, 91
short dancers and, 84, 87, 91,
111, 116
tall girls and, 67
toning body with Pilates and,
42, 170
Boston Ballet, 88, 97, 98, 99, 101,
171–73, 211

Boston Ballet Dancers Resource
     Fund, 173
Boston Ballet School, 96–97,
     99, 172
Boyd, Kirven J., *30*
Breakdancing, 50, 51–52, 54, 201
Broadway musicals, 54, 56, 81,
     137–38, 142, 193, 194,
     195–98
  agents and, 187
  backstage peek at, 139
  being lead in, 138, 197–98
  chorus dancing in, 193
  The Color Purple, 161–62
  dancer profiles, 47–56, 129–39,
     153–62, 189–98
  Fosse, 137, 138
  good and bad points of being in,
     54, 193
  Movin' Out, 54–56, *55,* 137, *137,*
     138, 139, 197–98
  Never Gonna Dance, 192, 197
  open calls for, 187
  switching from ballet to, 54–56,
     137–38
  "triple threat" abilities and,
     195–96
Brown, Clifton, 21, *22–23,* 23–32,
     28, 30, 33, 57, 126, 215
Brown University, 99–100, 101
Burnout, 4, 50, 98–99
Business side of career, 157
  agents and, 182, 187
Byrd, Donald, 133, 135, 160,
     161, 211

C
California State University, 155–56
Career Transition for Dancers,
     199, 213

Casting:
  agents and, 182, 187
  company class and, 172
  see also Auditions
Catanach, Daniel, 73, 74
Catharsis, 158
Character, getting in, 16, 42, 64
Character (folk) dancing, 33, 91
Cher, 154, 161, 163
Chicago, 198
Chicago City Ballet School, 85–86
Choreographers:
  classes taught by, 196
  dancers working as, 53, 139, 151,
     180, 186, 199
Chorus Line, A, 194, 198
Chuck E. Cheese's restaurants, 180
Cinderella, 11, 37
Classes. *See* Dance classes; Summer
     dance programs
Clothes, for auditions, 173, 182
Co.Dance Conventions, 175, 211
College education, 20, 29, 31–32,
     64, 67–69, 88–89, 91, 99–101,
     105, 112–13, 117, 124–26,
     133, 158, 168–72, 194
  dance companies with programs
     for, 20, 29
  majoring in dance and, 88–89,
     112–13, 158, 168–70
  modern dance and, 88–89,
     99–100, 105, 112–13, 117
Color Purple, The, 161–62
Columbia City Ballet (S.C.),
     15–16
Combination-learning abilities:
  auditioning and, 32, 91, 108, 120
  moving up to front row and, 108
  music videos and, 120
  reversing combinations and, 86, 91

Commercials, 158, 184, 194, 195
   auditioning for, 182–84
Companies. *See* Ballet companies;
   Modern dance companies
Company class, 18, 31, 32, 78, 116,
   126, 172
   before performances, 92, 163
Competitions. *See* Dance competitions
Competitiveness of dance world,
   18, 24, 26, 32, 62, 127, 135,
   172, 179, 193–94
Concertino, 77
Confidence, dancing with, 41, 66
Contemporary ballets, 80, 149
Contraction and release, 89, 105, 203
Contracts, negotiating, 187
Core, strengthening, 66
Corella, Carmen, 81
Corps de ballet:
   of American Ballet Theatre,
      19–20, 53
   of Boston Ballet, 172–73
   good and bad points of being in,
      73, 172
   of Houston Ballet, 42
   of New York City Ballet, 65–66,
      73, 78, 80, 147
Corrections, in classes, 26, 76, 116,
   144, 151
Corsaire, Le, 49, 57
Creative movement, 10, 33, 60, 84,
   201
Cross-training, 40, 110, 116, 126
Cry, 27

D
Dance classes:
   adagio in, 38
   in auditions and competitions,
      29, 32, 63, 126, 173
   barre work in, 12, 76
   company class, 18, 31, 32, 78, 92,
      116, 126, 163, 172
   corrections in, 26, 76, 116,
      144, 151
   finding work through contacts
      in, 102, 183, 196
   learning combinations in, 86, 91
   modern, for ballet dancers,
      17, 33, 36, 105
   moving up to front row in,
      32, 108
   studio-switching and, 14–16,
      21, 25, 62, 64, 85, 86,
      108, 110, 142–43, 146,
      179, 181
   types taken by dancers in this
      book, summary lists, 9, 23,
      35, 47, 59, 71, 83, 95, 107,
      119, 129, 141, 153, 165,
      175, 189
Dance companies. *See* Ballet
   companies; Modern dance
   companies
Dance competitions, 18, 24, 26,
   127, 179, 193–94
   ACT-SO, 157–58
   good and bad points of, 18, 26,
      127, 179
Dance criticism, 64
Dance magazine, 16, 112, 199, 213
Dance Theater of Harlem, 38–39
Dance/USA, 213
Dandelion Wine, 115
De Vita, Franco, 12, 33, 105, 173
Dirty Dancing, 181, 184
Disco dancing, 48, 202
Donald Byrd/The Group, 211
   see also Byrd, Donald
Dressers, 139

Drowned World Tour, 160–61
Dunham, Katherine, 203

E

Eating before performances, 56,
    84, 112
Eating disorders, 87, 93
    resources for, 213
Edgy look, 183, 195
Eliot Feld's Ballet Tech, 211
Ellington, Duke, 133
Esplanade, 113
Evans, Albert, *145,* 148
Expressive side of dance, 16, 20,
    24, 32, 41, 42, 64, 120, 131,
    144, 155, 156, 157–58, 168,
    191, 198
    arm movements and, 27
    creative movement classes and, 33
    getting into character and,
        16, 42, 64
Extension, 38

F

Faber, Rima, 117
Fancy Free, 79
Feet, 38, 41, 75
    dancing barefoot, 110, 112
    pointe work and, 11, 75, 81,
        131–32
Feld, Eliot, 135, 211
Figure skating, 96
Flamenco, 91, 202
Floor-Barre, 126
Florez, Nick, *174–75, 175–86, 178,
    185,* 187, 199, 215
Flower boy, 52
Folk (character) dancing, 33, 91
Fordham University, 29
Fosse, 137, 138

Fosse, Bob, 137, 202
Fouettés, 14
Freelance dancers, 43, 91, 102, 114
Friedman, Brian, 186
From Old Seville, 91
Front row of class, moving to, 32, 108

G

GED (General Educational
    Development) test, 75
Gloria, 85
Glover, Savion, 181, 203
Gordon, Lauren, 199
Graham, Martha, 105, 203
Grant, Lauren, *82–83, 83–93, 85, 90,
    98,* 102, 104, 117, 163, 195
Guys and Dolls, 195
Gym, working out at, 31, 32, 40,
    67, 80, 126
Gymnastics, 86, 154–55, 156, 157,
    161, 166, 190–91, 193,
    197–98
Gyrotonics, 18, 116

H

Haiku, 145, 148
Handel, George Frideric, *103*
Hard Nut, The, 91–92, 93, 98
Harlem Nutcracker, 133, 135, 161
Hayden, Melissa, 17
High school:
    alternatives to graduating from,
        75, 181–82
    arts-oriented, 16, 21, 29, 52–53,
        64–65, 74–75, 146
    editor of newspaper of, 99, 168
    regular high schools, 41, 62–65,
        87–88, 99, 123, 132, 144, 146,
        155–58, 167–68, 181–82, 194
    SAB students and, 64–65, 146

Hines, Gregory, 181
Hip-hop dancing, 51, 202
Hollywood. *See* L.A./Hollywood
    dance scene
Horton, Lester, 105, 203
Houston Ballet, 36, *37*, 40, 41,
    42–43, 45, 81, 212
  academy/school of, 33, 36–37, 40,
    81, 93, 105, 127
*How to Succeed in Business Without
    Really Trying,* 195, *196*

I
Improvise, 150, 177, 183
In a Word, 159
Indiana University, 117, 151,
    169–70, 171
Injuries:
  career-ending, 117, 199
  coping with, 6, 31, 110
  preventing, 40, 93, 116
Interlochen Arts Academy
    (Mich.), 21
International Conference of Blacks in
    Dance, 157, 160

J
Jackson, Janet, 176, 180, 184, 202
Jackson International Competition,
    18
Jacob's Pillow dance festival (Mass.),
    100–101, 112
Jazz dancing, 24, 25, 32, 33, 36, 72,
    78, 80, 120, 122, 135, 142,
    143, 147, 170, 179, 182, 202
Jealousy, 62, 190, 193–94
Jewels, 67, *68,* 147
Joffrey, Robert, 132–33, *134*
Joffrey Ballet, 132–35, 212
Joplin, Scott, *22*

José Mateo Ballet Theatre, 97
Juilliard, 124, 125–26

K
Kelly, Gene, 180, 203
Kelly, Sean, 37
King, Alonzo, 149–50, *150,* 211
Kirov Ballet, 57
Knitting, 146
Kostritzky, Olga, 73–74, 76

L
L.A./Hollywood dance scene,
    181–86, 187
  agents in, 182, 187
  auditions in, 182–84
  good and bad points about being
    in, 181
Late starters, 72, 75, 81, 105,
    130–34
Lemenager, Nancy, 187, *188–89,*
    189–98, *192, 196,* 199
Leventhal, David, 88, 92–93,
    94–95, 95–104, *98, 103,* 105
Limón, José, 105, 203
LINES Ballet, 148, 149–51,
    150, 211
Living Proof Farewell Tour, 161
Locatelli, Pietro, 115
Locke, Jill, *159*
Long, Doug, 21
Long Island University, 20
Los Angeles. *See* L.A./Hollywood
    dance scene
Losing, dealing with, 26, 125, 179,
    184, 194
Love Stories, 202
Lula Washington Dance Theatre,
    156–57, 158, 212
Lyrical dancing, 142, 202

M

Madonna, 160–61, 180, 181, 202

Marcovici, Sébastien, *145*

Mark Morris Dance Group, 88,
    91–93, 101, 102–4, 163, 212
  school of, 92, 104
  see also Morris, Mark

Mazzo, Kay, 81, 93, 127

McKenzie, Kevin, 19

Meet Me in St. Louis, 195

Midsummer Night's Dream, A, 67, 144

Miss Dance of New England, 194

Modern dance companies:
  being in, 26, 88, 110
  freelance dance jobs in, 102
  see also Alvin Ailey American
    Dance Theater; Mark Morris
    Dance Group; Paul Taylor
    Dance Company

Modern dancing, 17, 20, 29, 32,
    33, 36, 67, 78, 81, 87–89, 91,
    99–102, 105, 112–14, 117,
    203
  ballet central to, 113
  college education and, 88–89,
    99–100, 105, 112–13, 117
  dancer profiles, 23–32, 47–57,
    83–93, 95–104, 107–16,
    119–27, 129–39, 141–51,
    153–62
  starting age for, 105
  switching from ballet to, 88–89,
    99–100, 111–12

Moore, Rachel, 199

Moroccan Project, The, 150

Morphoses/The Wheeldon Company,
    151, 212

Morris, Mark, *85,* 88, *90,* 91–93,
    98, 101, 102–4, *103,* 212

Morris, Victoria, 5, 187, 199

Motherhood, dancing and, 43,
    45, 138

Movies, with dancing, 36, 48, 177,
    180–81

Movin' Out, 54–56, *55,* 137, *137,*
    138, 139, 197–98

Mozart Dances, 90

MTV, 120

Murphy, Gillian, 6, *8–9, 9–20, 11,
    13, 15,* 21, 57, 69, 117, 127,
    163, *200,* 215

Musical instrument, learning as a
    kid, 9, 23, 35, 37–38, 83, 86,
    95, 97, 107, 111, 119, 153,
    155, 166

Musicals. *See* Broadway musicals

Music videos, 81, 120, 180, 195,
    202
  auditioning for, 182–84

N

NAACP, 157

National Dance Education
    Organization (NDEO), 213

National Eating Disorders
    Association, 213

National Institute of Mental Health
    (NIMH), 213

Nervousness:
  advice for handling, 25, 87, 131
  in audition or performance
    situations, 25, 62–63, 87, 114,
    131, 132
  perfectionism and, 131

Never Gonna Dance, 192, 197

New York City Ballet, 6, 17, 45, 48,
    50, 52, 62, 63, 64, 65–69, 72,
    73, 75–76, *77,* 78, *79,* 80,
    117, 130, 142, *145,* 147–49,
    151, 212

New York City Ballet (*cont.*)
  apprentices with, 65, 75, 78–80,
    147
  corps de ballet of, 65–66, 73, 78,
    80, 147
  school of. *See* School of American
    Ballet
New York City Ballet Workout 2, 147
New York University (NYU),
    88, 199
  Tisch School of the Arts,
    88–89
Nissinen, Mikko, 69, 127, 171–72,
    173
North Carolina School of the Arts,
    16, 17–19
Nutcracker, The, 4, 17–18, 19, 29,
    36, 45, 48, 50, 63, 65, 72, 80,
    84, 85, 86, 91, 93, 97, 98, 99,
    101, 110, 114, 122, 123, 132,
    133, 135, 142, 144, 148, 161,
    166, 171, 184, 195
  Byrd's version of (*Harlem
    Nutcracker*), 133, 135, 161
  Morris's version of (*The Hard
    Nut*), 91–92, 93, 98
Nuts and Crackers, 195

O
Olympics, 190
Open calls, 187
Oprah Winfrey Show, The, 176
Ortega, Kenny, 184

P
Pain, coping with, 6, 69, 78,
    110, 112
Parkinson, Elizabeth, 54, 81,
    128–29, 129–39, *134, 136,
    137,* 151, 197, 198, 199

Parsons, David, *28*
Paul Taylor Dance Company, 87,
    100, 113–16, 163, 212
  school of, 88, 113–14
  see also Taylor, Paul
Pennsylvania Ballet, Rock School of,
    63, 76
Perfectionism, 131, 144, 151
Performances:
  backstage peek at, 139
  being in constant state of
    preparation for, 56
  being well prepared for, 16, 25,
    56, 89, 131, 163, 176
  company class before, 92, 163
  coping with pain and muscle
    tightness after, 6, 69, 78,
    110, 112
  eating before, 56, 84, 112
  evening, typical day with,
    112, 162
  getting into character for,
    16, 42, 64
  love for, 32, 67, 71, 80, 104, 108,
    116, 120, 144
  nervousness with, 25, 62–63, 87,
    114, 131, 132
  videos of, 12, 26–29, 51, 57, 64,
    75, 113, 215
  warming up before, 50, 163
Person, Melanie, 117, 151
Petipa, Marius, *49*
Physical therapy, 6, 31, 78,
    110, 112
Pilates, 40, 42, 89, 100, 116, 126,
    138, 163, 170, 197, 199
Pointe shoes, sewing ribbons on, *136*
Pointe work, 10, 11, 81
  late start in ballet and,
    81, 131–32

Port de bras (arm movement), 27
Post-performance careers, 5, 67, 92,
    104, 117, 139, 186, 198,
    199, 213
Power, Shelly, 33, 81, 93, 105, 127
Principal dancers in ballet
    companies, 14, 20, 43
  good and bad points of, 14
Private Domain (Taylor), 87
Prix de Lausanne, 18
Puberty, 93
Push-ups, 126

R
Ramasar, Amar, *70–71, 71–80, 77,*
    81, 122, 195
Reichlen, Tess, 6, 33, *58–59, 59–69,*
    61, 68, 163
Rejection, dealing with, 26, 125,
    179, 184, 194
Relationships in dance world, 183
Revelations, 27, *121,* 123
Robbins, Jerome, 77, *79,* 202
Roberts, Keith, 138
Robinson, Bill "Bojangles," 203
Rock School (Philadelphia),
    63, 76
Rocky, 24
Romeo and Juliet, 98
Royal Academy of Dance (London),
    99, 122
Russian style of ballet, 85, 86

S
Sales, Doricha, 117, 151
Saturday Night Fever, 48, 202
School of American Ballet (SAB),
    16–17, 40, 48–53, 63–65,
    73–76, 78, 81, 93, 117, 127,
    144, 146–47

auditioning for, 51, 63
  program to encourage boys to do
    ballet at, *70, 73–74*
  style of ballet taught at, 64, 75
  summer program of, 16, 63–64,
    69, 73, 144, 146
School of Ballet Arizona (Phoenix),
    25–26
Selena, 184
Selya, John, *2, 4, 46–47, 47–56, 49,*
    55, 57
Shining Star, 28
Short dancers, 53, 84, 87, 91,
    111, 116
Sims, Glenn Allen, 26, *30, 118–19,*
    119–27, 121, 125, 215
Sims, Linda Celeste, *121*
Singing, 38, 155, 162, 195–96
Singin' in the Rain, 36, 180
Sleeping Beauty, 39, 42, 84, 98,
    111
Small dance companies:
  good and bad points of, 148
Smallwood, Dwana Adiaha, *30*
Smiling while performing, 41, 75
Soccer, 10, 12, 50, 60, 62, 97
Soloists, 19, 20, 42, 66, 67
  good and bad points of being, 67
  understudies for, 66
Solomons, Gus, Jr., 199
Southern Methodist University
    (SMU), 158–60, *159*
Spears, Britney, 184
Spectrum Dance Theater, 211
Springfield Ballet (Ill.), 108–12, 114
Star mentality, 127
State Fair of Texas (Dallas), 176–77
Staying Alive, 177
Stevenson, Ben, 41, 42
Stiefel, Ethan, *15, 20*

Stiefel and Stars, 20
Story, Jamal, *152–53, 153–62, 159,*
    163, 187, 195, 215
Stravinsky, Igor, 77
Stretching, 89, 112
Studio-switching, 14–16, 21, 25,
    62, 64, 85, 86, 108, 110,
    142–43, 146, 179, 181
Styles of dancing, definitions, 201–3
    see also specific styles
Summer dance programs, 16, 20,
    31, 42, 62, 63, 69, 73, 76, 88,
    91, 99, 100–101, 112, 123,
    133, 144, 146, 181
    creating one's own, 168
Superstar tours, 154, 160–61,
    184, 186
    good and bad points of, 154
Surfer on the River Styx, 54
Survival jobs, 102, 110, 114, 197
Swan Lake, 12–14, *13, 15,* 16, 20, 42
Swayze, Patrick, 181
Sweet Charity, 198
Swimming, 10, 48, 126
Sylphide, La, 2, 4
Symphony in C, 66

T
TADA!, 72
Tallchief, Maria, 85
Tall-girl parts, 67
Tap, 181
Tap dancing, 24, 33, 58, 60, 72, 78,
    108, 120, 122, 142, 143, 147,
    176, 179, 191, 203
Taylor, Paul, 87, 88, 100, *109,* 110,
    112, 113–16, *115,* 160, 203,
    212
Taylor-Corbett, Lynne, *159*
Taylor 2 company, 114

Tchaikovsky, Pyotr, *61*
Teaching dance, by book's featured
    dancers, 20, 43, 56, 92, 104,
    139, 172, 186, 199
Teasing of boys for dancing,
    25, 50, 74
Temp work, 102, 114
Tharp, Twyla, 53–56, *55*
Tice, Julie, 5, *106–7, 107–16, 109,
    115,* 117, 163
Times They Are A-Changin', The, 56
Tisch School of the Arts (NYU),
    88–89
Touring, 88, 89, 110, 148
    good and bad points of, 26, 88,
    110, 148
    superstar tours and, 154, 160–61,
    184–86
Travolta, John, 48, 177
Tremaine, Joe, 181–82
Triple threat, 195
Trusnovec, Michael, *109*
Truth or Dare, 181
Turnout, 75, 81, 131
Types:
    hiring decisions and, 183–84
Typical day, 18, 31, 89, 100, 112,
    162, 176

U
Understudying roles, 65, 110
University of Michigan, 112–13
Unwinding, dance as strategy for,
    168
Urban Ballet Theater, 74, 212

V
Videos, 180
    of dance performances, 12, 26–29,
    51, 57, 64, 74, 113, 157

featuring performances by dancers
    in this book, 215
  see also Music videos
Visualization, 87
Vivaldi, Antonio, *85*

W
Walker, Alice, 161
Warming up:
  barre work in, 12, 163
  before performances, 50, 163
Washington, Lula, 156–57, 158,
    160, 212
Water intake, 56, 89
Weight training, 31, 126
Welch, Stanton, 81
Wheeldon, Christopher,
    151, 212

White Nights, 180
Wigs, 139
Wise, Scott, 138
Wood, Donna, 26–27
Working out, 31, 32, 40, 67,
    80, 100, 126
Writing:
  for dance solo, 157
  as a future career, 104
  in a journal, 171, 173
  for newspapers, 99, 158, 168
  poetry, plays, stories,
    154, 172, 177
Wroth, Sarah, *164–65,* 165–73,
    167, 169

Y
Yoga, 112, 116, 138, 163, 199

Printed in the USA
CPSIA information can be obtained
at www.ICGtesting.com
LVHW091132150724
785511LV00001B/91